KT-119-165

The Impact of Family Violence on Children and Adolescents

Javad H. Kashani
Wesley D. Allan

Volume 37
Developmental Clinical Psychology and Psychiatry

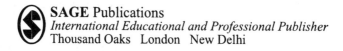

SAGE Publications
International Educational and Professional Publisher
Thousand Oaks   London   New Delhi

Copyright © 1998 by Sage Publications, Inc.

All rights reserved. No part of this book may be reproduced or utilized in any form or by any means, electronic or mechanical, including photocopying, recording, or by any information storage and retrieval system, without permission in writing from the publisher.

For information:

SAGE Publications, Inc.
2455 Teller Road
Thousand Oaks, California 91320
E-mail: order@sagepub.com

SAGE Publications Ltd.
6 Bonhill Street
London EC2A 4PU
United Kingdom

SAGE Publications India Pvt. Ltd.
M-32 Market
Greater Kailash I
New Delhi 110 048 India

Printed in the United States of America

Library of Congress Cataloging-in-Publication Data

Kashani, Javad H., 1937-
  The impact of family violence on children and adolescents / Javad H. Kashani and Wesley D. Allan.
    p. cm. — (Developmental clinical psychology and psychiatry; v. 37)
    Includes bibliographical references (p.) and index.
    ISBN 0-7619-0897-8 (cloth). — ISBN 0-7619-0898-6 (pbk.)
    1. Family violence—Psychological aspects. 2. Abused children--Mental health. 3. Abused teenagers—Mental health. 4. Victims of family violence—Mental health. I. Allan, Wesley D. II. Title. III. Series.
    RJ507.F35K37 1997
    616.85'822—dc21   97-33814

98 99 00 01 02 03 10 9 8 7 6 5 4 3 2 1

Acquiring Editor:	Jim Nageotte
Editorial Assistant:	Kathleen Derby
Production Editor:	Michele Lingre
Production Assistant:	Denise Santoyo
Typesetter/Designer:	Danielle Dillahunt
Cover Designer:	Candice Harman

98000395

362.8

Date Acq: AE 33-17

T

on Children
and Adolescents

23. A

Don

Developmental Clinical Psychology and Psychiatry Series

Series Editor: Alan E. Kazdin, Yale University

Recent volumes in this series . . .

8: LIFE EVENTS AS STRESSORS IN CHILDHOOD AND ADOLESCENCE
by James H. Johnson

9: CONDUCT DISORDERS IN CHILDHOOD AND ADOLESCENCE SECOND EDITION
by Alan E. Kazdin

10: CHILD ABUSE
by David A. Wolfe

11: PREVENTING MALADJUSTMENT FROM INFANCY THROUGH ADOLESCENCE
by Annette U. Rickel and LaRue Allen

12: TEMPERAMENT AND CHILD PSYCHOPATHOLOGY
by William T. Garrison and Felton J. Earls

13: EMPIRICALLY BASED ASSESSMENT OF CHILD AND ADOLESCENT PSYCHOPATHOLOGY SECOND EDITION
by Thomas M. Achenbach and Stephanie H. McConaughy

14: MARRIAGE, DIVORCE, AND CHILDREN'S ADJUSTMENT
by Robert E. Emery

15: AUTISM
by Laura Schreibman

18: DELINQUENCY IN ADOLESCENCE
by Scott W. Henggeler

19: CHRONIC ILLNESS DURING CHILDHOOD AND ADOLESCENCE
by William T. Garrison and Susan McQuiston

20: ANXIETY DISORDERS IN CHILDREN
by Rachel G. Klein and Cynthia G. Last

21: CHILDREN OF BATTERED WOMEN
by Peter G. Jaffe, David A. Wolfe, and Susan Kaye Wilson

22: SUBSTANCE ABUSE IN CHILDREN AND ADOLESCENTS
by Steven P. Schinke, Gilbert J. Botvin, and Mario A. Orlandi

23: CHILD PSYCHIATRIC EPIDEMIOLOGY
by Frank C. Verhulst and Hans M. Koot

24: EATING AND GROWTH DISORDERS IN INFANTS AND CHILDREN
by Joseph L. Woolston

25: NEUROLOGICAL BASIS OF CHILDHOOD PSYCHOPATHOLOGY
by George W. Hynd and Stephen R. Hooper

26: ADOLESCENT SEXUAL BEHAVIOR AND CHILDBEARING
by Laurie Schwab Zabin and Sarah C. Hayward

27: EFFECTS OF PSYCHOTHERAPY WITH CHILDREN AND ADOLESCENTS
by John R. Weisz and Bahr Weiss

28: BEHAVIOR AND DEVELOPMENT IN FRAGILE X SYNDROME
by Elisabeth M. Dykens, Robert M. Hodapp, and James F. Leckman

29: ATTENTION DEFICITS AND HYPERACTIVITY IN CHILDREN
by Stephen P. Hinshaw

30: LEARNING DISABILITIES
by Byron P. Rourke and Jerel E. Del Dotto

31: PEDIATRIC TRAUMATIC BRAIN INJURY
by Jeffrey H. Snow and Stephen R. Hooper

32: FAMILIES, CHILDREN, AND THE DEVELOPMENT OF DYSFUNCTION
by Mark R. Dadds

33: ADOLESCENTS AND THE MEDIA
by Victor C. Strasburger

34: SCHOOL-BASED PREVENTION PROGRAMS FOR CHILDREN AND ADOLESCENTS
by Joseph A. Durlak

35: CHILDHOOD OBSESSIVE COMPULSIVE DISORDER
by Greta Francis and Rod A. Gragg

36: TREATING CHILDREN AND ADOLESCENTS IN RESIDENTIAL AND INPATIENT SETTINGS
by Robert D. Lyman and Nancy R. Campbell

37: THE IMPACT OF FAMILY VIOLENCE ON CHILDREN AND ADOLESCENTS
by Javad H. Kashani and Wesley D. Allan

CONTENTS

Series Editor's Introduction   ix

Preface   xi

1. Definition and Nature of Family Violence   **1**
Definition of Family Violence   2
Nature of Family Violence   4

2. Etiology of Family Violence   **6**
Biological Perspective   6
Sociobiological Theory   7
Intergenerational Transmission   8
Family Systems Approaches   10
Parental Alcohol Abuse   13
Parental Personality Factors and Psychiatric Disorders   14
Summary   16

3. Caregiver Violence Toward Children   **18**
The Impact of Caregiver Violence on the Child   19
Physical Injury   20
Cognitive Functioning   21
Externalizing Problems   22
Internalizing Problems   24
Parent-Child Attachment and Child Social Development   28
Sibling Violence   30
Summary   31

4. Child Witnessing of Family Violence   **33**
The Nature of Spousal Violence   33

Etiology of Spousal Violence 34
Impact of Witnessing Spousal Violence on Children 35
Externalizing Problems 37
Internalizing Problems 37
Social Development 39
The Extreme Case: Spousal Homicide 40
Elder Abuse 41
Summary 44

5. Psychological Maltreatment Within the Family 46
   Etiology and Prevalence of Psychological
   Maltreatment 47
   Impact of Psychological Maltreatment
   on Children and Adolescents 48
   Summary 49

6. Cross-Cultural Perspective 50
   Patterns of Violence in Other Cultures 50
   Spousal Violence 52
   Violence Toward Children 52
   Violence Toward Elders 53
   Perceived Effects of Family Violence 53
   Societies Without Violence 54
   Summary 55

7. Assessment Strategies 56
   General Child Assessment 56
   Assessment of Degree of Child Abuse 57
   Assessment of Degree of Child Witnessing
   of Family Violence 57
   Assessment of the Impact of Family Violence
   on the Child 58
   Family Assessment 62
   A Word on Validation of Family Violence 63
   Summary 64

8. Intervention Strategies for the Violent Family 65
   Legal Responses 66
   Treatment of the Perpetrator 67

Treatment of the Child Who Has Been Abused
Within the Family 70
Treatment of the Child Who Has Witnessed
Family Violence 73
Family Therapy for the Violent Family 76
Summary 80

9. The Resilient Child and Prevention Strategies 81
Lessons From the Resilient Child 81
Prevention Strategies 82
Summary 85

10. Discussion and Future Directions for Research 86
Discussion 86
Problems and Future Directions for Research 87

References 91

Index 103

About the Authors 111

SERIES EDITOR'S
INTRODUCTION

Interest in child development and adjustment is by no means new. Yet only recently has the study of children and adolescents benefited from advances in both clinical and scientific research. Advances in the social and biological sciences, the emergence of disciplines and subdisciplines that focus exclusively on childhood and adolescence, and greater appreciation of the impact of such influences as the family, peers, and school have helped accelerate research on developmental psychopathology. Apart from interest in the study of child development and adjustment for its own sake, the need to address clinical problems of adulthood naturally draws one to investigate precursors in childhood and adolescence.

Within a relatively brief period, the study of psychopathology among children and adolescents has proliferated considerably. Several different professional journals, annual book series, and handbooks devoted entirely to the study of children and adolescents and their adjustment document the proliferation of work in the field. Nevertheless, there is a paucity of resource material that presents information in an authoritative, systematic, and disseminable fashion. There is a need within the field to convey the latest developments and to represent different disciplines, approaches, and conceptual views in the topics of childhood and adolescent adjustment and maladjustment.

The Sage series **Developmental Clinical Psychology and Psychiatry** is designed to serve uniquely several needs of the field. The series encompasses individual monographs prepared by experts in the fields of clinical child psychology, child psychiatry, child development, and related disciplines. The primary focus is on *developmental psychopathology*, which here refers broadly to the diagnosis, assessment, treatment, and prevention of problems that arise in the period from infancy through adolescence. A working assumption of the series is that to understand, identify, and treat problems of youth, we must draw on multiple disciplines and diverse views within a given discipline. The task for individual contributors is to present the latest theory and research on various topics including specific types of dysfunction, diagnostic and treatment approaches, and special problem areas that affect adjustment. Core topics within clinical work are addressed by the series. Authors are asked to bridge potential theory, research, and clinical practice, and to outline current status and future directions. The goals of the series and the tasks presented to individual contributors are demanding. We have been extremely fortunate in recruiting leaders in the fields who have been able to translate their recognized scholarship and expertise into highly readable works on contemporary topics.

In this book, Javad Kashani and Wesley Allan examine the impact of family violence on children and adolescents. The authors cover multiple forms of family violence, including abuse toward spouses, children, and elders, psychological maltreatment, and the witnessing of violence. The authors convey the interrelations, commonalities, and broad impact on the child. The book is remarkable in its coverage of theory, research, and clinical and legal issues. Theories regarding etiological views, research on the effects and underpinnings of violence, and efforts to intervene to treat as well as to prevent violence are well developed. Critical issues confronting the field are raised as well, including the advances and limitations in assessing violence and questions that have been neglected in research. Many excellent topics are integrated into the discussion to place violence in context. As one example, patterns of violence in other cultures are discussed, including countries without violence. Cross-cultural perspectives are critically important in light of the different forms, prevalence, views, and meanings or interpretations of family violence. The book is broad in its scope, detailed in its coverage, and engaging in style. Current research is interspersed with case studies to convey details about the tragedy of abuse and its consequences. The book draws on the remarkable research and clinical experience of the authors on a topic that is clinically and socially critical.

—*Alan E. Kazdin, PhD*

PREFACE

Violence within the family increasingly is identified as a profound societal problem that can exert a multitude of short- and long-term effects on youngsters and can take a variety of forms including abuse perpetrated by parents or siblings. Additionally, vicariously observing familial violence, such as spousal abuse, has documented untoward sequelae on children and adolescents. In an earlier paper we wrote on the topic of family violence (Kashani, Daniel, Dandoy, & Holcomb, 1992), we explained that "it is important to note at the outset that no single behavioral or emotional reaction epitomizes the abused child" (p. 183). Nevertheless, a plentitude of research has been conducted that attempts to elucidate relationships between different types of family violence, varying child characteristics, and the resulting impact of this violence on the child. This interplay of variables will constitute the main focus of this book.

In Chapter 1, the book will commence with a discussion regarding the definition, history, and societal costs of family violence. Chapter 2 will present a delineation of various proposed theories concerning the etiology of family violence as well as documentation for these frameworks. In Chapter 3, an exploration of the impact of intrafamilial violence directed toward youngsters by caregivers and siblings will be considered. Child witnessing of varying types of family violence will be the focus of Chapter 4, which will discuss spousal and elder abuse. Chapter 5 will consider a different type of family violence that can also be extremely destructive: psychological maltreatment.

Additionally, to provide a contrast to the current conditions in the United States, Chapter 6 will present a cross-cultural exploration of family violence. Chapter 7 will explore available assessment procedures, and Chapter 8 will examine intervention techniques. Chapter 9 will recount the "resilient child" and lessons learned from this type of youngster. Prevention strategies are also explicated in this chapter. Future research directions will be described in

Chapter 10 to aid mental health professionals and researchers who address the needs of this population.

This book will address primarily physical and verbal/psychological violence within the family. Sexual abuse and child neglect constitute other significant forms of child abuse, but these topics are beyond the scope of the current review. We would also like to note that, throughout the book, cases we have seen in our clinical work will be described to help illustrate particular points. For the purposes of confidentiality, the names and identifying data of these children and their families have been altered.

This book was made possible by the research of numerous individuals who are cited throughout the text. We would like to thank these researchers and encourage them and future scientists to continue to address the important topic of family violence. Wesley Allan also wishes to thank his research and professional mentors (in alphabetical order), Dr. Debora Bell-Dolan, Dr. Javad H. Kashani, and Dr. Christopher A. Kearney, for their help and encouragement through the years.

1

DEFINITION AND NATURE OF FAMILY VIOLENCE

All happy families resemble one another;
every unhappy family is unhappy in its own way.

—Tolstoy, *Anna Karenina*

The Robinsons were one such unhappy family. Helen Robinson was a 5-year-old girl who was referred to us for trichotillomania (hair pulling) that had resulted in several bald patches on her head. Her parents, Carol and Steven, were married, and both were successful professionals. Carol had a doctorate and Steven was in business. They considered themselves to be responsible parents and they did not understand why their daughter was behaving in this way. The parents appeared to care a great deal about Helen; in fact, Carol even seemed to like Helen better than Helen's sibling, Jason, who was 9 years old.

We conducted a detailed interview with Helen and discovered that one of her major concerns was the arguments that occurred between her parents. When we asked the parents about this arguing, they admitted that, for the last 2 years, they had occasional quarrels, but asserted that the children were not present at the time. Additionally, although the parents had considered divorcing approximately 18 months ago, they seemed to have worked out their problems and were committed to maintaining their marriage.

Carol then related to us that Helen had discussed several of her dreams with her mother. In these dreams, Helen's bedroom was on fire and the fire gradually spread throughout the house. Helen told her parents about the fire,

1

but they did not do anything. As a result, the fire continued to spread to the neighborhood and eventually engulfed the entire town. While reporting them to us, Carol indicated that she was embarrassed that she had initially missed the significance of these repetitive dreams and had not taken Helen's distress more seriously.

We met with the parents three times and educated them about the powerful impact that their arguments can have on their children. Carol and Steven acknowledged that they were careful not to fight in front of the children but were sometimes sarcastic or brusque with each other. In addition, they occasionally would have loud disagreements in their bedroom that could be overheard by Helen and Jason. We recommended that Carol and Steven make overt attempts to display their respect for each other in front of the children. They also made sure that the family did more pleasant activities together to facilitate a relaxed familial environment.

After this family intervention, Helen's hair pulling decreased dramatically and then stopped completely in a few months. This case study helps highlight the fact that children can be adversely affected by parental arguments, even without the presence of severe physical aggression. These quarrels were causing Helen to have anxiety regarding her future, which she apparently attempted to relieve by pulling out her hair. Fortunately, Helen was a bright and verbal young child who was able to articulate her concerns to us, and her parents were highly motivated to seek treatment and make active changes in their lives to help their child.

This example illustrates the impact that even family arguments may have on children. This pattern of heterogeneity in family violence is the norm. All kinds of families commit all kinds of violent acts that exert all kinds of effects on youngsters.

DEFINITION OF FAMILY VIOLENCE

An official definition of child abuse was drafted in 1974 as part of the Federal Child Abuse Prevention and Treatment Act (PL 93-237): the physical or mental injury, sexual abuse, negligent treatment, or maltreatment of a child under the age of 18 by a person who is responsible for the child's welfare under circumstances that would indicate that the child's health or welfare is harmed or threatened thereby. As can be seen, psychological maltreatment can be part of the constellation of child abusive behaviors.

Regardless of the fact that a national definition has been set forth, great inconsistency is noted when *abuse* or *family violence* are defined and operationalized by various researchers (Gelles, 1987b). Emery (1989), for example, suggests that whether an act is judged "abusive" or "violent" is based on multiple factors, including the form of the act itself, the impact on the victim, the intent of the aggressor, situational influences, and community standards. Thus social judgments become a part of the study of violence and help make the notion of a standardized definition more elusive (Emery, 1989).

Definitions of *violence* have been even more mercurial and equivocal, typically referring to any type of physical act that is aggressive or malevolent and intended to harm a person (Gelles, 1987b). However, this definition would include acts such as spanking a misbehaving child that may be somewhat more legitimate in nature (Gelles, 1987b; Kashani et al., 1992). Daniel and Kashani (1983) have defined *violence* as "mistreatment, injury, insulting and coarse language; to hurt by treating badly" (p. 709). Similarly, Gelles and Straus (1979) describe it as "an act carried out with the intention, or perceived intention of physically hurting another person" (p. 550).

Other authors (e.g., Newberger, Hampton, Marx, & White, 1986) have greatly broadened the concept of family violence by constructing a category called "pediatric social illness" and including physical violence, accidental injury, failure-to-thrive, and poisoning. It is assumed that these behaviors are abusive because they do not occur in families with a competent parent (Klerman, 1993). Consider the story of Jenny, who was a 26-year-old mother. One evening, Jenny put her two young children in the tub for a bath and left them alone for a few minutes while she finished emptying the dishwasher. The older child, Mark, who was 3 years old, decided that the bathtub needed more water, so he turned on the hot water faucet. The younger child, who was only 9 months old, was sitting directly below the faucet and began to cry as she was burned. Mark tried to turn off the faucet but was unable to do so. The baby was so badly burned before Jenny was able to get her out of the tub that she was in critical condition for three days and eventually died. Following the definition set forth by Newberger and colleagues (1986), Jenny is an abusive parent.

By definition, *family violence* includes abusive and violent acts of one family member against another member of the family. However, today's family often consists of a variety of people not related biologically, such as step-relatives. Another example is violence toward a child enacted by the boyfriend of the child's mother. The term *family violence* has a wide variety of meanings but, in its most basic form, generally refers to violent or abusive behaviors in the home directed toward one or more persons. This definition will be used for the purpose of this book. Additionally, the terms *abuse* and *family violence* will be considered equivalent because we will be referring to physical and violent acts.

NATURE OF FAMILY VIOLENCE

Child maltreatment was a widely accepted phenomenon for many centuries justified by the contention that child discipline needed to be maintained, even if harsh corporeal punishment had to be used (Radbill, 1974). The first scientific documentation in the literature of the negative effects of child abuse did not occur until 1962 with the publication in the *Journal of the American Medical Association* of a revolutionary article by Kempe and his colleagues (Kempe, Silverman, Steele, Droegemueller, & Silver, 1962), "The Battered-Child Syndrome." Within this framework, the "battered child" was one who sustained serious physical abuse, particularly from an adult caregiver. It was noted by the authors that this condition frequently went undiagnosed or was mishandled by professionals due to hesitancy to report such violence to authorities. The effects on society of this scientific report were phenomenal. Child abuse soon became a topic openly discussed in the literature as well as the media (Newberger, 1991) and has continued to be a hot topic.

To our knowledge, the first documented use of the phrase *family violence* in relation to children occurred in the early 1970s with the appearance of "Youth, Violence, and the Nature of Family Life" (Havens, 1972) in *Psychiatric Annals*. Havens proposed that the increasing knowledge regarding child abuse within the family signals that medical and mental health professionals should "abandon some of [the] idealization of family life and accept that parents not infrequently want to injure or even kill their children" (p. 20).

This initial and tentative work with child abuse in the early 1960s subsequently led to laws designed to protect children from violence as well as mandatory reporting laws for mental health professionals and others who have contact with children (e.g., teachers, physicians). Additionally, the identification of other types of family violence, including spouse and elder abuse, that may be witnessed by children has received a great deal of attention (Kashani et al., 1992).

Our information base concerning the problem of family violence has increased exponentially since the appearance of these seminal works. Today, researchers and clinicians working with children and families are well aware of the notion that children are abused and witness significant violence at a staggering rate in their homes.

The prevalence of family violence, however, is questionable because it is of a sensitive nature and likely to be hidden (Yegidis, 1992), a problem referred to as the "iceberg phenomenon" (Osuna, Ceron, Banon, & Luna, 1995). Additionally, the lack of a standardized definition across studies has hampered attempts to ecumenically assess the prevalence of family violence. Likewise, the costs of family violence are difficult to ascertain. Obviously, the most significant costs to society due to family violence are the direct and indirect impact on children and adolescents in the form of physical and psychological trauma. As such, these effects will be considered in depth in Chapters 3, 4, and 5.

From a pragmatic viewpoint, however, other costs of violence exist at a community and societal level that merit mention in passing. A plethora of health professionals are employed around the country to aid victims of family violence. Perhaps most notable among these professionals, due to their constant proximity to the problem, are employees of local and national Divisions of Youth and Family Services and other such child agencies. Thousands of persons are employed simply for the purpose of taking phone calls on national abuse hot lines. Additionally, numerous law enforcement agencies get involved and address the issue of family violence on a daily basis. Shelters house women and children who flee violent family environments.

Of course, helping victims of family violence should be a priority, and dollar costs seem inconsequential in comparison with the suffering of children and adolescents who have been abused or live in violent families. Nevertheless, if family violence could be eradicated, these staggering costs also could be obliterated. Further mention of this topic will be included in Chapter 9 when prevention strategies are contemplated.

2

ETIOLOGY OF FAMILY VIOLENCE

Given the complex nature of family violence, including its multitude forms, it comes as no surprise that a number of etiological models have been developed. We will review six frameworks that have gained the most attention: the biological perspective, sociobiological theory, the intergenerational transmission of violence, the family systems approach, parental alcohol abuse, and parental personality factors and psychiatric disorders. Spousal violence and its etiology are alluded to in this chapter but are considered in greater detail in Chapter 4.

BIOLOGICAL PERSPECTIVE

Violent behavior has been associated with a multitude of biological factors (Kashani et al., 1992), including genetic determinants, central nervous system malfunction, endocrine systems, epilepsy, neurotransmitters, chromosomal aberrations, and structural elements (Burrowes, Hales, & Arrington, 1988; Gunn & Bonn, 1971; Nielson, Christensen, Schultz-Larsen, & Yde, 1973). Neurotransmitters indicated in the development of aggression include serotonin, norepinephrine, dopamine, acetylcholine, and GABA (Yudofsky, Silver, & Hales, 1995). These chemicals appear to work in conjunction with one another to produce violence; however, low levels of serotonin and high levels of dopamine seem to be highly related to elevated aggression (Yudofsky et al., 1995).

Seriously violent male offenders have been found to have higher rates of prefrontal brain dysfunction, as marked by lower glucose metabolism, than a normal male nonoffender group (Raine, Buchsbaum, et al., 1994). Similarly, adults with a history of explosive episodes of rage were administered full neurological exams by Elliott (1982). The most common finding (36%) was minimal brain dysfunction (MBD), which is "a patchy or spotty distribution of cognitive perceptual, behavioral, emotional, motor, sensory, and reflex defects" (Elliott, 1982, p. 682) and stems from developmental or acquired organic disorders of the brain. However, because MBD can result in such a dizzying array of neurological symptoms and can have a variety of etiologies, drawing substantive conclusions from these data is difficult. There is also some evidence that criminal activity in men may be related to high plasma testosterone levels (e.g., Mattsson, Schalling, Olweus, Low, & Svensson, 1980; Schiavi, Theilgaard, Owen, & White, 1984). Kreuz and Rose (1972), for example, found that, among young aggressive prisoners, persons with histories of severe violence had a higher level of testosterone than prisoners without this same history. However, plasma testosterone levels were not different for men who had a history of fighting in prison versus those men who did not have this history. Thus the relationship between aggression and testosterone appears to be complex and mediated by other potential variables, such as childhood history, and researchers have not delineated the precise role testosterone may play in aggressive behavior (Burrowes et al., 1988).

In one of the few longitudinal studies available, Raine, Venables, and Williams (1990) examined a group of 15-year-old males from the general population in England and subsequent criminality rates at age 24 years. Of the 101 participants, 17 were found to have an official criminal record. These 17 males differed at age 15 years from their peers in terms of lower resting heart rate and skin conductance activity and greater slow-frequency electroencephalographic activity, which are indicative of autonomic underarousal.

Overall, however, the biological perspective of aggressive behavior seems to suffer from a lack of a unifying theory. Instead, it consists of relatively unconnected findings concerning the relationship between aggression and assorted biological functions or problems. Before this framework can be adequately applied to family violence, it would benefit from being consolidated. In addition, biological factors alone do not seem to fully account for the development of violence. Aggression seems to arise partly from genetic factors, but this relationship is influenced by the environment in which the individual is reared (e.g., Raine, Brennan, & Mednick, 1994; Raine, Brennan, Mednick, & Mednick, 1996).

SOCIOBIOLOGICAL THEORY

Sociobiological theories focus on the teachings of Darwin and the "notion that physical characteristics and behaviors of species develop over time through the process of natural selection" (Dutton, 1995a, p. 209). Using a sociobiological viewpoint, behaviors that help one's offspring survive are considered functional (Dutton, 1995a). Therefore, parents are expected to invest more resources in one of their own children than in a nonrelative child (Malkin & Lamb, 1994). The question that arises therefore is this: "How does family violence fit such a role?" Researchers have hypothesized that the sociobiological function of marital violence can be found in the potential purpose of "coercive control" in marriages, which can be viewed as being "motivated by the male need to guarantee his paternity by ensuring compliance through coercion" (Dutton, 1995a, p. 210). However, one of the major problems with this type of theory is difficulty in testing it in a systematic manner.

Theories that focus more broadly on the sociological variables in family violence attempt to link it to the broader social order (Levinson, 1989). For example, Garbarino (1977) points out that violent families tend to isolate themselves from a social support system. Additionally, these families often buy into societal beliefs that legitimize violence against children.

INTERGENERATIONAL TRANSMISSION

The intergenerational transmission of family violence has attracted a great deal of attention from theoreticians and empirical researchers. It involves the relationship between parental violence and subsequent child violence during adulthood. Specifically, "children are alleged to replicate the aggressive behaviors of their parents" (Cappell & Heiner, 1990, p. 135). Or, put another way, "abused children become abusers and victims of violence become violent offenders" (Widom, 1989, p. 160). Therefore, if a child's parents act aggressively toward each other or their children, then the child is later likely to act aggressively toward his or her spouse and children (Cappell & Heiner, 1990). As can be seen, this theory borrows heavily from theories of social learning.

This model first appeared in the literature as early as 1963 with the publication of a brief clinical note by Curtis (1963) in the *American Journal of Psychiatry* titled "Violence Breeds Violence—Perhaps?" Curtis invoked the popular phrase *Monkey see, Monkey do* to help explain his fledgling theory. From this early and tentative model has sprung the concept of the "cycle of abuse" (Cappell & Heiner, 1990) and the belief that "violence begets violence" (Widom, 1989; Yegidis, 1992).

A number of assumptions are implicit in this model, including the supposition that parenting techniques are learned from parents and that abused children become abusive parents. Exposure to violence is seen as a model that teaches a child to be abusive (Griffin & Williams, 1992). This subsequent violence appears to be an attempt from the prior victim to wield a sense of control over his or her life (Griffin & Williams, 1992). Some of these assumptions have been better documented than others. For example, parents who were abused as children tend to score higher on measures of abuse potential, such as the Child Abuse Potential Inventory, than parents who have not been abused (Milner, Robertson, & Rogers, 1990). Similarly, Rynerson and Fishel (1993) surveyed abusive parents participating in a treatment program and found that many of them had childhood memories of their fathers hitting their mothers (38.8% and 31% for males and females, respectively) and even their mothers hitting their fathers (29.4% and 28.4% for males and females, respectively). Additionally, most of the participants had been subjected by their parents to harsh disciplinary measures, such as being hit with something other than a hand (82.3% and 50.6% for males and females, respectively) and being hit with a closed fist (14.8% and 9.4% for males and females, respectively). Of course, retrospective data are always somewhat suspect and the parents may want to posit a reason for their abusive behavior; however, the amount of experienced and witnessed abuse is striking.

Kalmuss (1984) conducted a well-designed study on the effects on later violent behavior of witnessing or experiencing parental violence in childhood. In contrast to many other studies, which have not examined child witnessing separately from abuse, Kalmuss did separately analyze these forms of violence. The results supported the intergenerational transmission of violence in that both types of behaviors were related to subsequent marital violence in the next generation. However, observing familial violence was a stronger predictor than was being abused. This relationship was hypothesized to exist because, even though violence between any family members seems to convey the message that familial aggression is permissible, aggression between parents seems to teach the acceptability of later marital violence more readily than child abuse because, in effect, it matches the later behavior (i.e., spouse abuse) better. Alternatively, people may not view parent-child violence as aggression because of the prevalent nature of this behavior and because spanking is a widespread form of discipline. Thus it may not be seen as violence and cannot as easily serve as a model of violence to children.

A connection also has been found between abuse in youngsters and later criminal behavior (e.g., Lewis, Lovely, Yeager, & Femina, 1989). Widom

(1989) examined the connection between type of child maltreatment and later violence. Adults who experienced physical abuse as children were more likely to be arrested for a violent offense (15.8%) than children who encountered neglect (12.5%) or sexual abuse (5.6%). Adolescents in violent families also tend to adopt maladaptive coping styles that are similar to the methods used by their parents. For example, we (Kashani, Daniel, Sulzberger, Rosenberg, & Reid, 1987) found that adolescents with conduct disorder had a pattern of conflict resolution that tended to match their parents' modes of solving conflicts.

Results generally have supported intergenerational transmission theory; however, some studies have been sharply criticized due to methodological problems (Widom, 1989). Overall, though, this theory has attained a wide degree of acceptance in the mental health profession as well as the popular media (Widom, 1989). Kaufman and Zigler (1987) summarized the relevant research by concluding that "being maltreated as a child puts one at risk for becoming abusive but the path between these two points is far from direct or inevitable" (p. 190). Most children who are abused do not later become violent (Widom, 1989). A number of factors appear to moderate or mediate this relationship, including childhood resilience (which will be discussed in Chapter 9) and social support outside of the family. Thus the association between being abused or viewing family violence and consequently becoming abusive is "probabalistic, not deterministic" (Gelles, 1987a, p. 230).

FAMILY SYSTEMS APPROACHES

As we discussed in Chapter 1, violence against children in families was first identified in 1962 (Kempe et al., 1962) as constituting a problem. Gelles (1987a) points out that the first people to delineate a problem shape its subsequent development in the literature. Thus the fact that family violence has been approached primarily from an "individual level, medical/psychiatric perspective" (Gelles, 1987a, p. 229) is not surprising. However, gradually, several tenable family systems frameworks have evolved that emphasize that the problem is "situated between, and not within, individuals" (Willbach, 1989, p. 43). These various models thus stand in stark contrast to other theories explicated in this chapter.

Systemic theorists hypothesize that reciprocal social interactions that occur prior to acts of violence are of great importance and may serve to maintain violent acts. However, this view has been criticized by some authors because it assumes that family members have equality of power, which underplays the vulnerable nature of the victim and somewhat obscures in neutrality the fact that the perpetrator has caused harm (Flemons, 1989; Hurley & Jaffe, 1990; Willbach, 1989).

Many family systems approaches to family violence borrow certain aspects of the intergenerational transmission model. For example, the social interactional model examines the "reciprocal influences of family members' behavior" (Milner et al., 1990, p. 15). Specifically, physical abuse is assumed to occur based on parents' negative childhood experiences, such as abuse, and their own parenting and marital experiences. For example, parents who are violent toward their children report a great deal of marital discord and describe their children as aggressive and attention-seeking (Green, Gaines, & Sandgrund, 1974).

Another specific family systems model that has been applied to family violence is the Systemic Belief Approach. This model combines traditional family systems theory with individual and family beliefs (Robinson, Wright, & Watson, 1994). Specifically, it is speculated that, within violent families, family members hold certain beliefs (e.g., the acceptability of violence) that impede the family's ability to solve problems in an effective and nonviolent manner. Thus these families in conflict tend to have few facilitative beliefs that increase problem solving (Robinson et al., 1994).

Stress within the family also has been a source of research and posited as "the mechanism through which low socioeconomic status works to bring about child abuse" (Gelles, 1987a, p. 230). Parental unemployment, in particular, appears to be a tremendous stressor within a family and possible cause of violence toward family members (Bottom & Lancaster, 1981; Gelles, 1987a; Howell & Pugliesi, 1988; Jurich, 1990). For example, women who are battered tend to have unemployed spouses more often than control women (Appleton, 1980).

Barton and Baglio (1993) identified a number of additional factors associated with stress that may provoke violence toward children: troubles with adolescents, violence and separation, legal violations, work, family loss, financial strains, illness, public assistance, major changes in family situation, and young child management. Similar conditions have been examined by Bottom and Lancaster (1981), who pointed to stressors such as strained marital relations, unwanted pregnancies, crowded living environment, job dissatisfaction, and children with special needs including children born prematurely, children with mental retardation, or children with a chronic illness. Child temperament and difficult developmental periods like the "terrible twos" may be other, intra-individual child variables that contribute to a family's stress level.

The family systems literature also has explicated a number of individual parental characteristics that may be associated with abuse. These factors include role reversal whereby the parent depends on the child to gratify certain needs, parental impulse-control problems learned from viewing violence in their childhoods, low self-esteem, identity formation problems, defensiveness that aims to defend their low self-esteem, and scapegoating of the child (Green et al., 1974).

This last factor, scapegoating, deserves further attention as it is one that we have seen often in our clinical work. This scapegoating can be dangerous and may emanate from a number of sources, such as when a parent with spousal problems projects the spouse's negative qualities onto the child (Green et al., 1974) or when a child has characteristics that are disliked by the parents for whatever reason.

An example of scapegoating can be seen in the story of Kevin, whom we saw in our clinical practice. Kevin was 12 years old and came from a large family with five other siblings. A great deal of family violence was prevalent in his household. Some of it consisted of overt types of violence (including severe sexual abuse), but much of it consisted of psychological maltreatment. All of the children were abused in some manner, but Kevin seemed to be the recipient of the most brutal abuse and was blamed for many of the family's problems. Kevin's father seemed to have an intense hatred for the boy. In particular, he would become enraged when Kevin broke minor rules, such as staying outside past the 5 o'clock dinnertime. Several times after Kevin broke these trivial rules, his father doused him with gasoline and threatened to light him on fire. This chronic and severe pattern of abuse was eventually hotlined, and Kevin was removed from the home and placed in foster care.

Dysfunctional communication patterns within the family also have been posited as one possible origin of family violence. Bottom and Lancaster (1981) assert that "most abusive [family] members have not learned to talk about stressful circumstances, examine options for action, and decide on a plan for resolution" (p. 9). In contrast, physical forms of aggression are selected as methods of communication and modes of solving familial problems.

The constellation of the family also may influence the presence of family violence. For example, increasing evidence points to a relationship between single parenthood and increased abuse (e.g., Sack, Mason, & Higgins, 1985). This situation could be due either to having to raise children alone and the resulting difficulties or to economic hardship in the household (Gelles, 1989). The economic deprivation theory, however, has been best documented (e.g., Gelles, 1989). In particular, living with a poor, male single parent seems to place a child at high risk for being the victim of familial violence (Gelles,

1989). Adolescent mothers likewise have been considered to be at high risk for committing family violence because of the effects of poverty, limited education, and insufficient prenatal medical attention (Klerman, 1993). Additionally, young mothers may be more likely to unwittingly leave their children with an unfit and potentially abusive person, such as a young friend (Klerman, 1993).

In contrast, other studies have indicated that the likelihood of abuse increases with the presence of a stepparent or another "unrelated adult filling a parental role" (Wilson, Daly, & Weghorst, 1980, p. 333). Similarly, Osuna and colleagues (1995) found that having multiple families living together can lead to increased family violence.

A number of family systems frameworks have been delineated in the literature, but most focus on the pattern of relationships between family members that may cause or maintain violence. Maladaptive familial communication, in particular, seems common in families that are violent, and may serve as an important intervention target in the violent family (see Chapter 8).

PARENTAL ALCOHOL ABUSE

Some individuals use alcohol as permission and an excuse for their aggressive behaviors (Dutton, 1995a; Yegidis, 1992). The relationship between alcohol and violence in general has been examined in great detail, and there appears to be a fairly strong relationship between alcohol use and family violence (Appleton, 1980; Yegidis, 1992). However, this association seems to disappear once alcohol use becomes severe, perhaps because large quantities of alcohol act as an anesthetizing agent (Yegidis, 1992). Additionally, alcohol use seems to be more highly related to spousal violence than child abuse (Yegidis, 1992). Between spouses, alcohol consumption by either spouse can initiate an argument or reactivate habitual conflicts (Daniel & Kashani, 1983).

One woman with whom we worked became abusive in a manner that appeared to be directly related to her alcohol use. The mother was divorced and worked as a waitress in a local restaurant. She had a chronic problem with alcohol use but was generally a responsible mother. She made sure that her children always had enough to eat and clean clothes to wear to school. However, she would sometimes become violent with her boyfriend when they were out together drinking. On one occasion when she was drunk, she had an altercation with her boyfriend and returned home by herself. When she got home, she was extremely angry and her infant daughter started crying inconsolably. She later reported that her anger kept building and she hit her daughter one time. However, she used such force that the child suffered permanent vision impairment. Subsequently, all her children were taken out of the home and put into foster care, and the mother eventually went to prison briefly for her impulsive actions.

A notable critique of many studies investigating the relationship between aggression/family violence and alcohol use is their relatively simplistic methodological foundations. Specifically, the majority of them have focused on correlational analyses (see Murdoch, Pihl, & Ross, 1990). Thus variables that may serve roles as moderators or mediators of this relationship have been largely ignored. Bushman and Cooper (1990) conducted a meta-analysis of available studies and found that alcohol does appear to cause aggression, but the effects of alcohol were moderated by methodological factors, such as the nature of the control group.

A great deal of media attention has focused on spousal or child abuse as potentially deriving from drug or alcohol use/abuse. The data seem to confirm that although alcohol or drug use may be prevalent in some abusive families, the relationship between this factor and abusiveness is complex. Other factors, such as observation of marital violence in childhood, sex role egalitarianism, self-esteem, marital stress, and approval of marital violence, seem to play an etiologic role in family violence (Stith & Farley, 1993).

PARENTAL PERSONALITY FACTORS AND PSYCHIATRIC DISORDERS

The first etiologic model developed for family violence was the assumption that the abusive parent in violent families suffers from some form of psychopathology (Jurich, 1990). Treatment, therefore, focused on individual interventions for the parent who was mentally ill (Jurich, 1990). A variety of parental personality factors and psychiatric disorders have been linked to family violence and are referred to as "kind of person" models (Gelles, 1987a). For example, one of the most common diagnoses among individuals who commit family violence is antisocial personality disorder (ASPD). Persons with characteristics of ASPD, such as aggressiveness, rejection of social norms, and impulsivity, are assumed to engage in violence at relatively high rates (Daniel & Kashani, 1983).

Mothers who abuse their children appear to hold distorted cognitions with regard to their children and it is posited that these beliefs may contribute to family violence. For example, abusive mothers' attributions regarding their children's behavior tend to be internal and stable (Larrance & Twentyman, 1983). Thus they may be likely to view child misbehavior as being intentional and something that will recur. Larrance and Twentyman (1983) proposed a model based on these findings. In stage one, parents have unrealistic expectations for their child, such as expecting him or her to do chores that are developmentally inappropriate. In stage two, the child behaves in manner that is inconsistent with the parent's expectations, such as being unable to do the chores. In stage three, the parent misreads the situation and assumes that the child acted with malice and intentionally to annoy the parent. In stage four, the parent reacts by punishing the child, perhaps with harsh physical discipline.

Not surprisingly, hostility and stress also have been examined in relation to family violence. Men who are violent within the family have been found to exhibit greater indirect hostility, irritability, resentment, and verbal hostility than men who are not maritally violent (Barnett, Fagan, & Booker, 1991). Maiuro, Cahn, Vitaliano, Wagner, and Zegree (1988) compared three groups: men who have been domestically violent, men who have been generally assaultive, and a control group of nonviolent men. Higher levels of anger and hostility were found in the men who were domestically or generally assaultive in comparison with the control group. However, the group of men who exhibited family violence were more depressed than either the control group or the generally assaultive men. Thus depression may act as a moderator or mediator of the relationship between anger/hostility and violent behaviors within the family. Consistent with these findings, Dutton (1995a, 1995b) has postulated that abusiveness within the family by men is the result of their cyclical mood swings.

A small subsample of men who are violent within the family may have a more serious mental illness. Much of this work, recently, has been conducted in cases where the woman actually leaves the relationship and the man subsequently exhibits "stalking" behaviors (Meloy, 1996). Stalking is a profound problem that, even with a temporary restraining order legally in place, often has tragic results (Meloy & Gothard, 1995). In these cases, a diagnosis of de Clerambault syndrome, or the DSM-IV category (American Psychiatric Association, 1994) of delusional disorder, erotomanic type, seems appropriate (Meloy, 1996). These men do not usually have an overt mental disorder but often have a narcissistic personality type (Meloy & Gothard, 1995).

Parental psychotic behavior has also sometimes been linked to family violence directed toward children (e.g., Myers, 1970); however, this evidence has consisted largely of a few case studies and does not seem to adequately describe the majority of violent parents. Nevertheless, a case that we saw illustrates this occurrence. James was an 8-year-old boy who was hospitalized for aggressive behavior toward peers at school and oppositional behavior at home. His family life was marked by a great deal of chaos. His mother was a caring person and tried the best that she could, but she was unable to fully meet James's physical or emotional needs. James's father had been diagnosed with schizophrenia and was not particularly close to James. He worked at a sheltered workshop and functioned fairly well by taking antipsychotic medications. James was hospitalized for aggression when he was 6 years old and again at age 7. His aggressive behavior appeared to be fairly stabilized for more than a year; however, his conduct began to deteriorate and he was hospitalized for a third time. This third admission occurred after James's father stopped taking his antipsychotic medications. Apparently, his father started to experience psychotic symptoms, including paranoid ideation. James's mother reported that the father had been spending more time with James and was "telling him weird things," which seemed to bother James. Although the father did not become actively violent, his behavior severely affected James and the father's behavior therefore approximated psychological maltreatment.

Although a few parental personality characteristics have been delineated as likely causal factors in family violence, overall these models are viewed as relatively simplistic (Gelles, 1987a). Attaching a diagnosis (e.g., antisocial personality disorder) to a person who is violent may describe his or her behavior but adds little to the understanding of the genesis of the aggression. Other factors are assumed to be of importance apart from or in conjunction with personality traits or psychopathology. In particular, preexisting catalysts toward conflict within the family, such as poor communication or problem-solving skills, also may need to be present (Green et al., 1974). As a result, theories linking violence and personality factors largely fell out of favor in the 1970s and 1980s (Yegidis, 1992), and the association between the two is not strong (Monahan & Arnold, 1996).

SUMMARY

The field of research that has examined possible etiologic models of family violence has suffered from the assumption that it can be explained with a "single factor" explanation (Dutton, 1995b). The research to date seems to suggest that no single theory can fully account for the problem of family violence, and multiple etiologic pathways are indicated to help fully explain the multidimensional nature of family violence (Gelles, 1987a). Social learning and the intergenerational transmission of aggression, however, seem to be particularly powerful theories when attempting to explain the etiology of family violence. Although familial violence is a unique form of aggression, research has generally demonstrated that it develops much like any other type of violence (Wolfe & Jaffe, 1991). Thus many models of family violence are based upon or resemble more general models of aggressive behavior, whereas other models (e.g., intergenerational transmission, systemic theories) more fully take into account the distinctiveness of the family system. Future research would profit from combining various elements of existing theories with careful empirical documentation to develop an integrated paradigm that merges conceivably relevant components.

3

CAREGIVER VIOLENCE
TOWARD CHILDREN

Caregiver violence toward children, or family violence directed toward a child, consists of a variety of child abusive acts, including hitting, kicking, and beating with an object (e.g., a belt) that may leave marks or permanent tissue damage. This problem seems to cut across socioeconomic status (SES), educational level, race, and a number of other parent and child characteristics. Violence toward children does, however, appear to peak (or at least be reported more often) when children are between the ages of 3-4 and 15-17 years (Straus, Gelles, & Steinmetz, 1980). Younger children seem to be vulnerable because of their small size and lack of coping skills (Jurich, 1990). Adolescents, on the other hand, may provoke their parents by being oppositional or hitting back when being physically punished or abused (Jurich, 1990). Following the institution of the Child Abuse Prevention and Treatment Act in 1974, interest in child abuse within the family has increased dramatically (Kashani, Shekim, Burk, & Beck, 1987). A major topic of interest, and the main focus of this book, is the impact that such abuse exerts upon children who are abused within their families.

Initial research in this area was characterized by a number of methodological problems, including small samples, lack of control groups, questionable reliability of information provided by family members, and the use of nonstandardized assessment tools (Kilpatrick & Lockhart, 1991; Yegidis, 1992). From the time of the early studies that first identified child physical abuse as a potential problem, through today, a great deal of progress has been made in the literature. Studies that have been conducted recently employ careful definitions of abuse, multiple control groups, and multiple informants.

To facilitate the current discussion, this chapter will first review a few problems that have traditionally plagued the field with regard to the definitions of child abuse used across studies. Next, the varying types of common abuse sequelae will be described. Finally, we will examine a special case of family violence—sibling abuse—and its potential impact.

As we indicated earlier, there are a multitude of definitions used for *abuse* (Emery, 1989; Kashani, Shekim, et al. 1987). *Maltreatment* is the broad term used to denote any kind of negative or harmful behaviors involving a child. This umbrella category is subdivided into *abuse* and *neglect*. Abuse, which concerns us here, can be further partitioned into physical, sexual, and psychological (e.g., derogatory statements directed toward a child that are intended to hurt his or her feelings, exact retaliation, or lower self-esteem). Given the myriad terms, it is not surprising that there is some confusion in the field and the literature and that definitions of child abuse have "lack[ed] comparability, reliability, and taxonomic delineation" (Augoustinos, 1987, p. 16) across studies. Further, the effects on the child of these varying types of abuse are heterogenous in nature. Therefore, the careful definition of *abuse* is crucial in any meaningful discussion. For this chapter, we will define *abuse* as physical abuse of a child that is perpetrated by a family member (psychological maltreatment is discussed in Chapter 5).

THE IMPACT OF CAREGIVER
VIOLENCE ON THE CHILD

Although the actual episode of family violence is usually acute in nature, its consequences can be manifested in a variety of more chronic child responses (Wolfe & Jaffe, 1991). In general, no single reaction exemplifies the child who has been abused by a family member (Kashani et al., 1992). Family violence can result in a "complex developmental unfolding of possible psychiatric disturbance" (Famularo, Kinscherff, & Fenton, 1992, p. 864). The mechanism of impact on the child appears to be the disrupting influence that family violence has on the child's ongoing development (Wolfe & Jaffe, 1991).

A child's reaction to familial abuse may be moderated by a number of considerations such as support from other, nonabusing family members, premorbid intellectual level, and genetic factors (Kashani et al., 1992). Other aspects of a child's environment (e.g., lack of stimulation, poverty) may actually generate more negative effects than the ordeal of being a victim of violence (Augoustinos, 1987).

Several categories of child functioning will be examined in relation to violence directed toward children. These domains include physical injury, cognitive functioning, externalizing problems, internalizing problems, parent-child attachment, and child social development.

PHYSICAL INJURY

The most obvious and overt effect of family violence on a child is observable physical damage in the form of scars or other injuries (Herrenkohl & Herrenkohl, 1981). "Shaken baby syndrome," for instance, is a major cause of severe damage to children secondary to family violence. One father we interviewed for court evaluation had violently shaken his 9-month-old child when he was alone with the child, who had been crying inconsolably. As a result of this abuse, the child was blind and had severely limited motor movement.

Another child we treated was abused twice as an infant by two different perpetrators. At age 3 months, Curtis suffered a head trauma secondary to abuse by his biological father. At age 10 months, his mother's boyfriend abused Curtis, causing two skull fractures and a ruptured tympanic membrane. This history of abuse (and subsequent family chaos) has had serious consequences, and Curtis was psychiatrically hospitalized four times by the time he was 8 years old. His reasons for admission have included depression and social problems, and, due to the chronic nature of the family violence, he continues to have serious problems.

Of course, the most extreme case of child abuse eventuates in child homicide (Husain & Daniel, 1984). Unfortunately, this happens all too often and may occur when abused children are prematurely returned to the home (Hollander, 1986). Myers (1970) reported that, among 134 child murders between 1940 and 1965, 35 (26%) were perpetrated by the child's mother and 14 others (11%) were committed by the father or a father figure (e.g., stepfather). Of note, most of the mothers appeared to be psychotic, whereas the fathers were usually reacting with extreme rage to an instance of child misbehavior. Krugman (1983-1985) identified 24 children during a 2-year period who died as a result of fatal child abuse from a family member. Most of the children were 3 years or younger and more likely to be male. Head injuries were the most common cause of death. The most frequent "triggers" for the violence were a toileting accident, messy diapers, or unending crying.

COGNITIVE FUNCTIONING

For several decades, researchers have noted a potential connection between child abuse and mental retardation or impaired cognitive functioning. However, many early studies employed retrospective methods and lacked appropriate control groups (Sandgrund, Gaines, & Green, 1974), which therefore limited the ability to draw definitive conclusions and cause-and-effect relationships from available data (Augoustinos, 1987). The first controlled study was conducted by Sandgrund and colleagues (1974), who compared 60 children who had been physically abused, 30 children who experienced neglect, and 30 nonabused children. All children were administered either the Wechsler Preschool and Primary Scale of Intelligence or the Wechsler Intelligence Scale for Children. Results indicated that the abused and neglected children scored lower on the Full Scale IQ than the control group. However, the two maltreated groups did not differ from each other.

More recently, Hoffman-Plotkin and Twentyman (1984) examined the cognitive functioning of children who had been abused. The authors compared 14 children with a history of abuse, 14 children with a history of neglect, and 14 children with no history of maltreatment. Each child was administered a battery consisting of the Stanford-Binet Intelligence Scale, the Peabody Picture Vocabulary Test, and the Merrill-Palmer Scale of Mental Tests. Consistent with the findings of Sandgrund and colleagues (1974), children who had been abused or neglected scored lower on each cognitive measure than the control group, but the two maltreated groups scored similarly.

A case we saw illustrated the relationship between impaired cognitive functioning and family violence in a lamentable manner. Jacob was a normally developing 5-year old child who suddenly began exhibiting acting out behavior, including hitting peers and biting a teacher. His mother, cognizant that these types of behaviors were uncharacteristic for Jacob, assumed that he was reacting to the chaos in the home. She and her husband argued often and she recently had decided to divorce her husband. Jacob's behavior continued to deteriorate and she had him hospitalized. A full medical and neurological work-up was completed and the results were startling; Jacob's urine drug screen (UDS) was positive for high levels of arsenic. Although it was never conclusively proven, Jacob's father was suspected of poisoning him. We recently saw Jacob again at age 13 years; he was diagnosed with mental retardation and had an IQ of 33. Jacob was unable to do most developmentally appropriate tasks, including tying his shoes. His gait as well as fine and gross motor movement were impaired. Additionally, he had extremely poor social skills and had recently sexually acted out with a female peer in the bathroom at his day care facility.

Overall, children who are the targets of family violence seem to have lower subsequent cognitive functioning than their nonabused peers. This relationship may be due to head injury that results in trauma to the brain. On the other hand, children who have been abused do not tend to score differently on cognitive measures than children who have experienced neglect. Thus factors inherent in the homes or families where inadequate parenting occurs (i.e., abuse or neglect) may serve to dampen cognitive development. For example, both environments may be marked by low levels of stimulation and communication (Augoustinos, 1987). Additionally, Augoustinos (1987) has asserted that many of the developmental sequelae of physical violence actually may be attributable to undetected low levels of neglect, which may have a more profound effect. Of note, most studies that have examined the cognitive functioning of children who have been the target of violence have drawn primarily from a low-SES sample, which may bias results (Augoustinos, 1987; Nightingale & Walker, 1991).

EXTERNALIZING PROBLEMS

A large portion of studies examining the relationship between family violence and behavioral problems have focused on child witnesses of familial abuse as opposed to children who have themselves been abused (see Chapter 4 for details on this topic). However, it appears that children who experience violence tend to exhibit similar behavioral problems as children who witness violence within the family (Jaffe, Wolfe, Wilson, & Zak, 1986a).

Famularo and colleagues (1992) documented that maltreated children display ADHD and oppositional-defiant and conduct disorders at a higher rate than a psychiatric control group. The maltreated group, though, consisted of both children who had been abused as well as children who experienced neglect. These populations are different and ideally should be further subdivided to provide greater specificity.

One study that used this methodology was conducted by Jaffe and colleagues (1986a), who examined three groups: child witnesses, children who were abused, and a control group. The child witness group consisted of 32 children from a battered women's shelter who had witnessed family violence as indicated on the physical aggression subscale of the Conflict Tactics Scale. The group of children who were abused comprised 18 male children who had been physically abused by a parent and identified by a welfare agency. The control group included 15 children from the general community who were solicited via a newspaper advertisement. The three groups were administered the Child Behavior Checklist (Achenbach, 1991) and their scores were compared on the externalizing subscale. The three groups diverged from each other on the externalizing subscale, with the abused children scoring highest, followed by the child witnesses and control group children. Additionally, fully 90% of the children who had been abused scored at least one standard deviation above the mean for the scale's normative data compared with 75% of the child witnesses and 13% of the control group children. However, because the study sample of abused children consisted entirely of males, it is not clear what kind of behavioral problems may be exhibited by female children who have been abused.

Hoffman-Plotkin and Twentyman (1984) also separated abused and neglected children for analyses and found that abused children were rated as more aggressive by parents and teachers than average children. However, the abused and neglected children did not differ from each other on this dimension. We (Kashani, Daniel, et al., 1987) found that adolescents from a community sample who met criteria for a diagnosis of conduct disorder had been abused by their parents more often than adolescents without behavioral problems.

Aggressive behaviors following abuse thus appear to be relatively common. This relationship can be seen in 13-year-old Tom, whom we saw on an inpatient child unit. Following years of physical abuse by his father, Tom was taken out of the home and his father received 5 years in the penitentiary (the sentence also was for sexual abuse of Tom's older sister). The physical abuse usually consisted of severe beatings for Tom's minor misbehavior but also occurred when Tom's father was drunk. During one such incident, his father repeatedly tried to hit his feet with a hammer. Tom subsequently began displaying externalizing symptoms, including running away from foster placements, setting a barn on fire, and assaultive behavior toward peers and adults. He also had recently stolen a BB gun, a crossbow, a knife, and a flashlight, perhaps in anticipation of running away from home. When Tom became angry, he would hit his head against walls, put pins in his fingers, yell, and cuss. His misbehavior resulted in multiple placements for Tom. When we interviewed him, it became clear that he was a scared kid who acted out to cope with his fear. He described having frightening dreams and indicated his wish: "I want a killer dog for my pet." Tom seemed to feel unprotected after years of abuse and sought protection from any available source.

One possible explanation of the preponderance of behavioral problems among children and adolescents who have been abused is the effects of modeling. That is, abused children have experienced violence in the home and learn to act out to cope with problems. However, Jaffe and colleagues (1986a) posit that these behavioral problems could be a reflection of numerous other factors that could exist in violent families, such as family stress, lack of child social support, and inadequate parental child behavior management. Conversely, at least in some cases, the child's behavioral problems may actually incite familial maltreatment (Famularo et al., 1992). This interpretation is controversial but may partially describe some families, and thus merits further consideration in the literature.

INTERNALIZING PROBLEMS

Initially, studies of the psychological sequelae of familial violence on children focused primarily on behavioral and cognitive problems (Allen & Tarnowski, 1989). Gradually, however, emotional or affective problems have been examined in relation to abuse. In particular, child depression and anxiety disorders and symptoms appear to be affiliated with familial violence that is directed toward a child or adolescent, and they will be reviewed here.

Depression

Although a strong relationship has not been documented between family violence directed toward a child and a subsequent diagnosis of major depression in that child, many researchers have posited that children who are abused may exhibit many symptoms of depression. Kashani, Shekim, Burk, and Beck (1987), for example, found a significant relationship between children's self-reported fear of future abuse and a diagnosis of depression. Additionally, a number of clinical reports (e.g., Kashani & Ray, 1987) have documented that children who have been abused manifest symptoms of depression, such as sad affect, social withdrawal, and low self-esteem.

We saw Bobby, a 5-year-old boy, after his parents brought him to the emergency room because of his "personality changes." Specifically, he was often angry and broke the rules. During our assessment, Bobby and his parents reported that Bobby exhibited many depressive symptoms, including sad affect, poor appetite, anhedonia, and chronic fatigue. Additionally, Bobby had many strange thoughts that seemed related to chaos in the family. Specifically, Bobby's parents practiced extreme discipline measures: spanking him with a belt daily, yelling at him, placing him in a corner for long periods of time, and making him drink a mixture of vinegar and water. Bobby came to believe that his parents were trying to poison him and he was diagnosed with major depression with delusional features. It seemed that Bobby could no longer cope with the abuse in his family and subsequently became severely depressed (Kashani & Ray, 1987).

Kazdin, Moser, Colbus, and Bell (1985) tested the hypothesis that children who are abused may exhibit high levels of depression. Participants in their study consisted of 79 inpatient children (15 girls and 54 boys) who were hospitalized for a number of reasons, including aggression, suicidal behavior, and psychotic episodes. For the study, *abuse* was defined as "physical injury inflicted by a parent, guardian, or other adult responsible for the care of the child" (p. 300). One of the strengths of the study is that both the child and the parents were interviewed to determine the presence of abuse.

Of the 79 children, 33 children were identified as physically abused. The 46 children who had not been abused served as the control group. Children completed the Children's Depression Inventory (Kovacs, 1992), the Hopelessness Scale for Children (Kazdin, French, Unis, Esveldt-Dawson, & Sherick, 1983), and the Self-Esteem Inventory (Coopersmith, 1967). Results demonstrated that children who were physically abused had higher levels of depression and hopelessness and lower self-esteem than the nonabused control group. Children were also split into four groups: past abuse only, current abuse only, past and current abuse, and no abuse. Notably, the children with both past and current abuse scored significantly higher on the measures of depression and hopelessness and lower on the self-esteem measure than the three other groups. Thus it appears that children with a history of abuse who are still being abused may experience the most severe symptoms of depression, perhaps because of the "protracted history of helplessness and exposure to parental figures with diminished positive affective display and interaction" (p. 303).

This study was replicated in an outpatient sample by Allen and Tarnowski (1989), who found that, when compared with nonabused children, abused children reported more depressive symptoms, greater hopelessness, and lower self-esteem. Nevertheless, depression scores for the abused children were not in the clinical range and were lower than the scores found in the Kazdin et al. (1985) study, indicating that depression may be found primarily in the most disturbed sample of children who have experienced family violence.

The relationship between family violence directed toward a child and subsequent depression is frequently explained via the concept of "learned helplessness" (Seligman, 1975) whereby the noncontingent nature of the violence causes a child to feel helpless and consequently to develop depressive symptoms. Indeed, children whose families have been violent to them do report greater internal attributions than control children (Allen & Tarnowski, 1989). Therefore, they may view themselves as helpless against violence and, potentially, as causing the problems in their environment.

Of interest, although depression appears to have a moderate relationship to abuse, and sexual abuse is associated with suicidal ideation, physical abuse does not seem to be significantly related to suicidal ideation or suicide attempts among adolescents (Adams, Overholser, & Lehnert, 1996; Kaplan, Pelcovitz, Salzinger, Mandel, & Weiner, 1997). However, most clinicians can probably attest to seeing numerous children or adolescents who were abused and either attempted suicide or presented with suicidal ideation. For example, we recently treated a 9-year-old boy, Frank, who had been severely abused by his father in the past. Additionally, upon admission, he was observed to have many bruises on his body, and he reported that his mother had been hitting him with a flyswatter. Frank frequently responded to stress by banging his head on walls and referring to himself as a "bad boy." He would also make suicidal statements and made several self-harm attempts, such as cutting a fan cord and reporting that he was going to place the exposed wires in his mouth.

Post-Traumatic Stress Disorder and Anxiety

Some children who have endured familial violence may display a number of symptoms of post-traumatic stress disorder. Specifically, nightmares about the violence may occur and children may become anxious when the subject is discussed (Kashani et al., 1992). The full syndrome of post-traumatic stress disorder (PTSD) is frequently examined in relation to child sexual abuse. However, PTSD has not as often been studied systematically in child/adolescent victims of intrafamilial physical abuse (Pelcovitz et al., 1994).

Brandy, a 12-year-old female whom we treated on an inpatient unit, exemplifies the relationship between abuse and later PTSD. She was living with her mother, who had been diagnosed with schizophrenia, paranoid type, and five younger siblings. Her family was positive for marked family violence. Brandy's older brothers would frequently "punish" her by punching her repeatedly in the upper arm until she was bruised. Additionally, approximately 2 years before this hospitalization, Brandy's mother shot her boyfriend in the stomach, ostensibly because he called her a "whore." Although her mother claimed that Brandy was not in the room at the time, Brandy appeared to exhibit many symptoms of PTSD, seemingly related to witnessing and experiencing familial violence. For example, when placed in time-out, Brandy would react strongly by verbally threatening staff, and would later explain that she felt "cornered." When administered projective testing, Brandy's responses reflected a great deal of fear about bodily harm and she frequently talked about characters being beaten or shot in a drive-by shooting.

Of interest, Pelcovitz and colleagues (1994) conducted a well-controlled study of adolescent physical abuse and found that adolescents who had been physically abused did not experience a higher proportion of PTSD than adolescents in a normal control group. Additionally, the three participants in their study who had been physically abused and met criteria for PTSD reported the PTSD symptoms as emanating from extrafamilial sexual assault. However, the physically abused adolescents did exhibit higher rates of general internalizing problems.

One study (Deblinger, McLeer, Atkins, Ralphe, & Foa, 1989) even found slightly, but not significantly, lower rates of PTSD among physically abused inpatient children (6.9%) as compared with nonabused inpatient children (10.3%). The children who were physically abused did, however, exhibit more symptoms from the PTSD avoidance/dissociative subcategory. It should be noted that the authors used a retrospective methodology; when the study was replicated by Adam, Everett, and O'Neal (1992) without using retrospective reports, higher rates of PTSD in physically abused children were found (20% versus 6.9% in Deblinger et al., 1989).

Famularo and colleagues (1992) concluded that maltreated children are diagnosed with PTSD more often than psychiatric controls. In fact, fully 39% of the children in the maltreated group reported PTSD. As we mentioned previously in this chapter, though, the authors combined abused and neglected children in their sample, which limits the ability to determine the likelihood that a child who experiences family violence will later develop PTSD. In a later study, Famularo, Fenton, and Kinscherff (1993) included finer delineations among maltreated children and found that physical abuse, in contrast to sexual or emotional abuse, did not predict a diagnosis of PTSD.

Pelcovitz and colleagues (1994) suggest that physical abuse does not necessarily carry the same degree of secrecy and shame as does sexual abuse and therefore may not lead to PTSD as often as does sexual abuse. Specifically, physical abuse frequently occurs when corporal punishment becomes extreme (Jurich, 1990); because corporal punishment is socially acceptable to most people in our society, adolescents may not view physical abuse as something that is unusual. Physical abuse may therefore have a relatively neutral valence, in comparison with sexual abuse, and may not thus precipitate PTSD as easily (Pelcovitz et al., 1994).

PARENT-CHILD ATTACHMENT
AND CHILD SOCIAL DEVELOPMENT

Children in violent families often do not experience the warmth, affection, and caring from parents that is associated with healthy parent-child relations (Stone, 1996). The trust between a child and a violent parent may be severely strained (Johnson, 1979), and violence toward a child by a parent often serves to disrupt the development of child-parent attachment (Katsikas, Petretic-Jackson, & Knowles, 1996).

For example, females abused as children retrospectively report that their relationships with their parents were typified by an insecure attachment style (Katsikas et al., 1996). Developmental problems and psychopathology appear to be closely related to disruptions in the parent-child relationship that can be caused by parental aggression, and this interference may have a more negative effect on a child than the actual violence (Wolfe & Bourdeau, 1987). In violent families, the normal equilibrium between positive and negative interactions is not achieved (Wolfe & Bourdeau, 1987), which leads to an aversive environment that is not conducive to bonding between family members.

Not surprisingly, the relationship between parents who are abusive and their children differ in fundamental ways from the relationship between nonabusive parents and their children (Herrenkohl, Herrenkohl, Toedter, & Yanushefski, 1984). Specifically, Herrenkohl and colleagues (1984) reviewed the literature and found that abusive parents tend to initiate fewer interactions with their children. There also tends to be little physical contact between children and parents. Additionally, within interactions, there are more negative and fewer positive behaviors exhibited by parents or children. Abusive parents also are described as rejecting and showing little warmth.

In addition to overt violence, the aggressive family tends to live in an environment that fails to provide the children with appropriate opportunities for or models of socialization or bonding (Wolfe & Jaffe, 1991). Hence, it is not surprising that children who are victims of family violence often have impaired social relations. These relational problems could begin as early as infancy. For example, toddlers who come from stressed, but nonviolent, families tend to respond to distress (e.g., crying) displayed by age-mates by exhibiting concern, empathy, or sadness. In contrast, toddlers who have been physically abused by their parents tend to notice (e.g., look at) distress in age-mates but do not show empathy, concern, or sadness (Main & George, 1985). In some cases, they even strike out aggressively at the distressed child. The authors of this study (Main & George, 1985) point out that the conduct of the abused toddlers resembles the rejecting behaviors displayed by parents who are violent; these findings thus support the intergenerational transmission theory of family violence (see Chapter 2).

Among children, the social behavior of youngsters who have been abused by a caregiver generally is more disturbed than the social behavior of peers who have not been abused. One outstanding study that examines this relationship was conducted by Salzinger, Feldman, and Hammer (1993) and merits being described in detail as a model of family violence research.

The abused group consisted of 87 children who were physically abused and reported to the New York State Child Abuse and Maltreatment Register. Each child was matched with a nonabused peer from his or her classroom. Data were collected in the children's homes and classrooms from peers, teachers, and parents. Children who had been abused tended to have lower peer sociometric status and receive fewer positive peer nominations (e.g., Whom do you most like to play with?) and more negative peer nominations (e.g., Whom do you least like to play with?) than control children. Children who had been abused were less often classified as popular and more often classified as rejected or neglected than the nonabused control group. The authors point out that some children who were abused were categorized as popular, indicating that certain protective factors are likely to exist that help children avoid the social pitfalls often associated with familial abuse.

Peers in this study also rated abused children as exhibiting fewer prosocial behaviors (e.g., leadership, sharing) and more antisocial behaviors (e.g., fighting, meanness, attention-seeking) than nonabused cohorts. Of interest, a difference was not found between abused and nonabused children for shyness, indicating that children who have been abused may not be more socially inhibited or withdrawn than their peers. As expected, abused children received negative peer nominations from peers to whom they gave a negative nomination. However, children who were abused also sometimes received negative peer nominations from peers to whom they gave a positive nomination, which did not occur for nonabused children. Thus abused children may have children with whom they play, but they may not actually be liked by these children, and the friendship therefore is not fully reciprocated.

There is also evidence that children who are abused may actually view, form, and maintain relationships in a fundamentally different way than their nonabused cohorts. Specifically, abused children tend to have more insular friendships in that their friends were less likely to be known by their parents than were the friends of nonabused peers (Salzinger et al., 1993). This finding seems consistent with data from studies of abusive families indicating that insularity of the family from outsiders is common and perhaps even promoted

(Garbarino, 1977). Abused children are also more likely to befriend younger peers than are children who are not abused (Salzinger et al., 1993).

Children's play also may be affected by family violence. Specifically, children who have been physically abused by their caregivers, when put into a structured play activity (e.g., Lowenfeld World Technique), tend to be more active and less organized than children who have not been abused or who have experienced sexual abuse. Their play creations are also notably marked by fights, wars, and conflict (Harper, 1991). Thus it appears that children who are abused may be acting out in fantasy the violence that they have experienced in their homes.

Overall, it appears that children who experience abuse tend to have poor parent-child attachment and social relationships. These social disturbances may have important implications as they negatively affect the child's ability to access extrafamilial social support to help cope with current problems and family stress. Additionally, these problems could continue to affect the person through adulthood and impair future social support, intimate relationships, and occupational functioning.

SIBLING VIOLENCE

The importance of good sibling relationships to children's development has been emphasized, and relationships with siblings are usually among the longest relationships people have, outlasting parent-child relations (Jalongo & Renck, 1985). Siblings have many of the same experiences, and in healthy families, they can be good sources of support (Kashani, Mehregany, Allan, & Kelly, in press). However, in some families, sibling rivalry can lead to violence. In fact, some have argued that sibling rivalry is characterized by a desire to symbolically eliminate the sibling with whom one is competing for parental attention (Neubauer, 1983).

The high frequency of imitation and interaction among siblings suggests that this relationship is of great developmental importance. This includes both the direct impact of siblings and the effects of the siblings' relationships with their parents (Dunn, 1988). Of primary concern to parents and clinicians is the frequent aggression and conflict exhibited between some siblings (Baskett & Johnson, 1982). Several researchers have documented that sibling violence can play an important role in the development of aggressive behavior (Gully, Dengerink, Pepping, & Bergstrom, 1981; Patterson, 1984).

As with elder abuse, the impact of sibling abuse on children and adolescents is studied relatively infrequently, and results are inconclusive (Kashani et al., 1992; Kornblit, 1994). However, it does appear that coercive sibling behavior toward a target child is associated with impaired peer relationships. Richman, Stevenson, and Graham (1982) reported poor relationships with siblings to be more common in children with other behavioral problems than a control group. Specifically, they found that poor relationships with siblings at 4 years of age were related to other problems existing during that time and to a clinical rating of disturbance 4 years later.

Sexual and psychological abuse may also be inflicted by siblings, often without parental knowledge, and can result in many types of trauma (Kashani et al., 1992). In a few extreme cases, sibling violence can result in homicide (Kashani, Darby, Allan, Hartke, & Reid, 1997; Pfeffer, 1996).

SUMMARY

To date, a number of conditions have been invariably linked to parent-child physical violence that occurs in the family. These areas include impairment in social relationships and cognitive development as well as behavioral and emotional problems. A particular child may manifest any combination of deficits in these areas, and so the pictures that emerge of abused children are heterogeneous ones.

In addition to these common symptom patterns, some children may display a more idiographic reaction. We are reminded of Daniel, who experienced severe physical abuse from his father. Daniel was removed from the home and placed in foster care, and subsequently rarely saw his father or nonabusive mother. Daniel was not particularly close to his mother and, despite the abuse, generally preferred to be with his father. Following a period of acting out in a variety of ways in his foster home, Daniel was psychiatrically hospitalized. As part of his treatment, we recommended that his mother visit him; we hoped that the parent-child relationship could be strengthened. This impending visit seemed to create a great deal of anxiety for Daniel, which worsened as the visit drew nearer. When his mother arrived, Daniel indicated that he was glad to see her; however, he began to display signs of a conversion reaction. Specifically, he reported losing the ability to use his right arm, and his mouth became frozen partly open. As the visit progressed, Daniel seemed to become less anxious and eventually these conversion symptoms dissipated.

Although Daniel displayed some behaviors commonly associated with abuse, including aggression, his experience reminds us that the long-term effects of family violence are unpredictable and individual for all children and adolescents. One question that remains largely unanswered is how parent-child violence differentially affects these areas for specific children. Protective factors have been mentioned, including extrafamilial social support, but the moderating or mediating effects of such variables have not been examined. Thus it appears that the study of resilience (see Chapter 9) and protective factors may be beneficial and help researchers fine-tune their results.

4

CHILD WITNESSING
OF FAMILY VIOLENCE

This chapter will commence with a description of the phenomenon of spousal violence in terms of definition, prevalence, and etiology. The impact on children of witnessing spousal violence will comprise the next, and primary, section of the chapter. Spousal homicide, which we consider to be an extreme case of family violence, will then be discussed. Finally, the witnessing by children of elder abuse will be contemplated.

THE NATURE OF SPOUSAL VIOLENCE

Spousal violence, or the cycle involved in the battered woman syndrome, is a behavior pattern, characteristically inflicted on a female by a male, that occurs in physical, emotional, and psychological forms (Appleton, 1980; Kashani et al., 1992). Typically, *spouse* refers to a married person; however, in the case of spousal abuse, it can also be indicative of unmarried persons who cohabit or are in some other form of intimate relationship (Drake, 1982). For example, we have treated many children who reported witnessing their mother being beaten by a boyfriend or the child's grandfather. The objective of this violence is generally the need of the abuser to have greater power in interpersonal relationships (Dickstein, 1988). Spousal abuse is typically perpetrated by men, with women accounting for approximately 95% of all reported spousal violence victims (Tilden & Shepherd, 1987). Women who are abused suffer physically and psychologically and may require medical treatment or hospitalization (Rosenbaum & O'Leary, 1981a).

Most of the studies in this area focus on the "battered woman" who is "repeatedly subjected to any forceful physical or psychological behavior by a man in order to coerce her to do something he wants her to do" (Walker, 1979, p. xv). However, it is often stipulated, perhaps to differentiate chronic from acute situations, that this pattern must occur more than one time without the female ending the relationship for it to constitute "battering" in contrast to assault (Walker, 1979).

In the 1970s, interest in and awareness of spousal violence developed along with the rise of the feminist movement (Davis, 1988). In contrast to child abuse, society was relatively slow to recognize spousal abuse as a major problem (Kashani et al., 1992), and consequently women have traditionally not been protected adequately from abuse by legislation (Tilden & Shepherd, 1987).

Spousal abuse was once thought to occur relatively infrequently, but by the early 1980s, it became clear that the problem was ubiquitous (Rosenbaum & O'Leary, 1981a). In terms of prevalence, one in five adult women have reported witnessing at least one incident of physical abuse between their parents during childhood (Henning, Leitenberg, Coffey, Turner, & Bennett, 1996).

ETIOLOGY OF SPOUSAL VIOLENCE

A number of etiological models have been proposed in relation to spousal violence. Some of them have been described in Chapter 2 under the general rubric of family violence. However, a few theories have been advanced specifically for spousal violence. Walker (1979) and later Drake (1982) have outlined a model of spousal violence that posits three pertinent and relatively predictable phases.

In Phase 1, tension between the couple builds from minor irritations and disagreements. Minor battering, such as throwing objects or verbal abuse, transpires. The female may respond during this period by withdrawing or becoming passive to assuage the violence.

During Phase 2, the tension surpasses a point where it can be contained by the batterer and an acute episode of violence ensues, generally lasting 2-24 hours. Here, in contrast to Phase 1, the violence is marked by a total lack of control. Generally, the woman's only available responses are either to endure the abuse or to flee the situation. Her choice may be affected by the presence or absence of children. Commonly, the woman responds by physically withdrawing and this self-imposed seclusion frequently delays medical attention.

Phase 3 involves a more tranquil stage during which reconciliation occurs between the spouses; indeed, a "honeymoon" phase may ensue accompanied by profuse apologies, gifts, and promises to change from the batterer. However, Phase 3 inevitably subsides and tension builds as the couple cycles back into Phase 1, and the sequence of violence resumes.

Many researchers and theorists have also pointed to the possible modeling effects of witnessing spousal abuse in childhood or experiencing direct abuse as leading to spousal violence in adulthood (Rosenbaum & O'Leary, 1981a). In fact, husbands who are abusive do tend to retrospectively report higher rates of childhood abuse and to have witnessed spousal abuse in childhood more often than nonabusive husbands (Rosenbaum & O'Leary, 1981a, 1981b). Among adult men, self-reports of physical assault of their spouses are correlated with memories of being shamed as children by their parents (Dutton, van Ginkel, & Starzomski, 1995). These shaming behaviors include public humiliation and random, undeserved punishment. Female children who witness battering may learn that passive acceptance is admissible (Rosenbaum & O'Leary, 1981a). However, findings have not documented that abused wives tend to have witnessed parental violence as children, and more research is needed to better document these relationships in males and females.

Alcohol and alcoholism are also presumed to sometimes play a role in the origin and/or maintenance of wife abuse, and male batterers have been found to have higher rates of alcoholism than nonbatterers, at least by wives' reports (Rosenbaum & O'Leary, 1981a).

In terms of coping, battered women may attempt to change the spouse so as to continue the relationship, may abandon the relationship, or may become violent themselves (Kashani et al., 1992). In some extreme cases, a battered wife may become assaultive or homicidal (Moore, 1975). Notably, many interspousal murders are committed by the victims of spousal abuse (Daniel & Kashani, 1983; Kashani et al., 1992). These murders are usually committed in self-defense and without premeditation or malice (Daniel & Kashani, 1983).

IMPACT OF WITNESSING
SPOUSAL VIOLENCE ON CHILDREN

Researchers have persistently documented that marital or couples violence is commonly accompanied by child abuse (e.g., Suh & Abel, 1990); fathers who abuse their wives are also likely to hurt their children (McCloskey, Figueredo, & Koss, 1995; Rosenbaum & O'Leary, 1981a). This section will consider, as much as possible, the effects of child witnessing of marital violence independent of child abuse with the implicit understanding that teasing apart these forms of violence is difficult. Episodes of witnessing violence are typically conceptualized as incidents of parental conflict with the child in visual or auditory range (e.g., Jaffe et al., 1986a). The fact that spousal violence could generate negative sequelae in children was first examined in Moore's (1975) landmark article in *Child Welfare*. Tellingly, these child witnesses to spousal violence were referred to as "yo-yo children," which alludes to the pattern of dysfunctional parental interactions that leave the child figuratively suspended in midair like a yo-yo. These children were described as "jumpy," "anxious," and "nervy." Additionally, they tended to be scapegoated by their parents and had numerous school problems. However, the authors asserted that the most afflicted group comprised children who were used as pawns in their parents' arguments.

A few years later, these children were no longer described as "yo-yos" but were still considered "forgotten" (Elbow, 1982) or "unintended" victims (Hershorn & Rosenbaum, 1985; Rosenbaum & O'Leary, 1981b). By this time, the impact of spousal abuse was more fully comprehended, as expressed by Rosenbaum and O'Leary's (1981b) observation that wife battering exceeded alcoholism in terms of its prominence as a major health concern. Additionally, researchers had a more complex view of the possible consequences this problem could have on youngsters who witnessed spousal brutality, including the possibility that these children could "mature into the next generation of abusive husbands and abused wives" (Rosenbaum & O'Leary, 1981b, p. 693).

Only in the late 1980s, however, was child witnessing of spousal abuse recognized as a potential etiologic factor for child psychopathology and associated problems (Hughes, 1988). One reason that literature on the effects of marital violence on children has developed slowly may simply be due to the fact that, initially, the greater need for direct intervention with the parents and the abusing system overshadowed the possible impact on child witnesses (Davis, 1988). Further, due to the sensitive nature of the problem, conducting research in this area has often been difficult for mental health researchers. Indeed, most researchers have been forced to become adept at accessing these types of children in nontraditional settings, such as domestic violence shelters or women's shelters (Carlson, 1990).

Today, however, a plethora of research exists that examines the influence of spousal abuse on children. Nevertheless, documented differences between child witnesses of violence and control children from nonviolent families seem to depend on the particular factor or characteristic selected for evaluation (Kashani et al., 1992), and these children tend to be a heterogenous population (Wolfe & Jaffe, 1991). In general, though, researchers have examined a number of categories with some regularity. These categories, which will be reviewed below, include problems in externalizing, internalizing, and social development domains.

EXTERNALIZING PROBLEMS

Behavioral and externalizing problems have commonly been noted in child witnesses to violence between parents. Typically, studies in this area employ the Child Behavior Checklist (CBCL; Achenbach, 1991) and compare children in families with and without spousal violence (e.g., Jaffe et al., 1986a). In particular, preschool boys seem to be at risk for developing behavioral problems in cases where the parents are abusive to each other (Fantuzzo et al., 1991; Hughes & Barad, 1983; Stagg, Wills, & Howell, 1989). For example, anger and distress are commonly exhibited by young children whose parents engage in angry interactions (Cummings, Vogel, Cummings, & El-Sheikh, 1989).

School-aged and adolescent boys also appear to be at great risk for developing externalizing behaviors (Porter & O'Leary, 1980; Wolfe, Jaffe, Wilson, & Zak, 1985). For example, adolescent boys who witness parental violence have high rates of running away from home (Carlson, 1990). Of course, in this case, researchers should examine whether this type of behavior is oppositional or actually more adaptive than staying in a violent household. In the same study, it was also found that adolescent male witnesses to family violence often use physical violence with their mothers, including during conflict resolution (Carlson, 1990). Here, the effects of past modeling on current behavior seem obvious.

In an early study, Rosenbaum and O'Leary (1981b) found no differences in conduct disorder or personality disorder symptoms between children of violent couples and children in two control groups (i.e., nonviolent couples with discord and satisfactorily married couples). However, they had a relatively small sample that consisted entirely of males, which may have obscured any significant relationships.

INTERNALIZING PROBLEMS

Internalizing reactions to the witnessing of violence can include anxiety and depression. Again, the CBCL is the most commonly used instrument and includes an internalizing factor that combines elements of anxiety and depression (Achenbach, 1991). Internalizing problems tend to be elevated among preschoolers from violent families residing in a shelter in comparison with children from violent families who still reside in their homes (Fantuzzo et al., 1991) or with comparison to normative figures (Hughes & Barad, 1983). Of interest, Stagg and colleagues (1989) found increased internalizing problems on the CBCL for preschool boys, but not for preschool girls. The findings that preschool boys more typically develop internalizing problems in response to observing parental violence is initially somewhat unexpected due to previous statistics showing that females are more likely to exhibit anxiety or depression (APA, 1994) and males are more likely to act out. However, it appears that males exhibit more of both kinds of behavior in response to witnessing family violence (Jaffe, Wolfe, Wilson, & Zak, 1986b). Thus males generally seem to experience greater levels of overall problems in relation to witnessing spousal abuse.

Among children who have witnessed spousal violence, some internalizing symptoms, particularly depression, may emerge due to the effects of modeling. Victims of violence, such as women who are battered by a spouse, sometimes tend to engage in a process of self-blame with regard to the aggression (Cascardi & O'Leary, 1992). This pattern of self-blame could culminate in feelings of depression if the violence were to continue. For example, Cascardi and O'Leary found that, among a sample of women who were battered, 52% scored in the severe range of depressive symptoms on the Beck Depression Inventory (BDI; Beck, Rush, Shaw, & Emery, 1979) and, as the level of violence increased, BDI scores were correspondingly elevated.

Symptoms of anxiety also may be displayed by children or adolescents who witness spousal violence. We are reminded of a recent clinical case we saw in which a child witnessed his mother being beaten by his father once prior to his parents' divorce. Five years later, when he was 17 years old, the adolescent was generally well functioning. He participated in sports, received good grades, and intended to attend college on a sports scholarship. However, he presented at our clinic with chronic anxiety problems. In particular, he felt an almost overwhelming need to protect his mother and experienced anxiety in relation to this task. Even though overt family violence occurred only once, this child was dramatically affected and his behavior continued to be directed by this incident for many years. Of course, his witnessing of parental arguments also may have affected his emotions; however, he specifically pointed to the beating as something that he remembered and that bothered him a great deal.

Suicidal thoughts may also emerge in youngsters, primarily male adolescents, who witness marital/couples violence (Carlson, 1990). These findings are consistent with the "lockage phenomenon," which proposes that in conflicted or abusive families, an adolescent may be under such intense and relentless pressure, either from abuse or witnessing of abuse, that he or she can see only two possible means of escape: suicide or homicide (Mohr & McKnight, 1971; Post, 1982). In our own research (Kashani, Darby, et al., 1997) with juveniles who committed intrafamilial homicide, we found high rates of family violence. Further, the homicide frequently followed an unsuccessful suicide attempt, which was perhaps an effort to escape from the family violence.

SOCIAL DEVELOPMENT

Problems in social relations and competency are another area examined in conjunction with child witnessing of spouse abuse. Preschoolers and children from homes with physical violence score lower or more impaired on measures of social competency than youngsters in nonviolent homes (Fantuzzo et al., 1991; Wolfe, Zak, Wilson, & Jaffe, 1986). Children who temporarily reside in a shelter with their abused mothers are particularly likely to exhibit impaired social competence, perhaps due to the unfamiliar setting, presence of many strangers, and lack of comforting possessions, such as toys (Fantuzzo et al., 1991). These effects, however, may be primarily situational, and long-term follow-up of these children is needed before more unequivocal conclusions can be derived.

Long-term effects of witnessing family violence also have been noted in the area of child social development. For example, women who report that they were witnesses, as children, to physical conflict between their parents tend to display more social maladjustment, including a lack of perceived social support, poor attachment to significant others, and a sense of impoverished social integration, than a comparison group (Henning et al., 1996).

A Caveat Regarding Research
Conducted in Shelters

A salient methodological problem with the extant literature of child witnessing of violence is the oversampling of research participants from battered women's shelters. This population represents a unique cross section of persons who witness family violence; however, it may constitute the most severely affected children and adolescents. Groups with less acute abuse may display concurrent diminished levels of internalizing and externalizing problems. In addition, living in a shelter seems to have a unique influence on children, especially with regard to their social interactions, which may be independent of the experience of family violence (Fantuzzo et al., 1991).

Wolfe and colleagues (1986), for example, compared children currently in a shelter, children who formerly lived in a shelter, and a control group, and found that the children in the shelter had the poorest social adjustment. Residing in a shelter, even temporarily, may thus be a child risk factor, and researchers should identify ways to make shelters more child friendly. Additionally, adolescents are typically unlikely to accompany their mothers to such shelters, perhaps preferring to stay with friends or relatives (Carlson, 1990). Thus, to access information pertaining to the impact on adolescents of vicarious observation of violence in the home, researchers may have to look to settings that may have larger populations of adolescents who have previously witnessed violence between their parents, such as residential homes or foster care (Carlson, 1990).

THE EXTREME CASE:
SPOUSAL HOMICIDE

Perhaps the most horrendous instance of family violence occurs when one parent kills the other (Burman & Allen-Meares, 1994). As we noted earlier, homicides do sometimes occur in an intimate relationship (Rosenbaum & O'Leary, 1981a) and are often preceded by considerable spousal violence. When one spouse murders the other, a child automatically loses both caretakers due to the death of one and the imprisonment or hospitalization of the other (Black, Harris-Hendriks, & Kaplan, 1992; Black & Kaplan, 1988; Burman & Allen-Meares, 1994). It is also common for the parent who committed the murder to subsequently commit suicide (Black & Kaplan, 1988). Following the murder, the child is frequently removed from the home and placed in foster care (Black & Kaplan, 1988).

If the child directly witnesses the murder, is in the home at the time, or observes the aftermath (e.g., the body, blood), development of symptoms or the full syndrome of post-traumatic stress disorder (PTSD) is common (Black & Kaplan, 1988; Pynoos & Nader, 1990) and may include intrusive thoughts, nightmares, increased arousal, and emotional detachment (APA, 1994). Apparently, though, PTSD generally tends to emerge in these cases only if the child was present in the home during the murder, perhaps due to the necessity of a visual or auditory stimulus to become the focus of flashbacks and so forth.

In some cases, children have been left alone with or have to seek emergency assistance for the victim (Black et al., 1992), which could be traumatic for most children. Similarly, anxiety-related symptoms could develop due to fears of, among other things, being killed by the parent or having to interact or live with the murderer in the future. Swift intervention with these children is generally recommended (Black & Kaplan, 1988) and will be described in Chapter 8 (see PTSD).

Another possible consequence of spousal violence is pathological bereavement in a child or adolescent (Black & Kaplan, 1988; Black et al., 1992). The feelings of sadness due to loss of a parent may be compounded by feelings of horror and shame associated with the murder (Black & Kaplan, 1988). Great stigma may be placed on the children of a murderer (Black & Kaplan, 1988) and media attention in such cases may be unavoidable. Self-esteem may be diminished for such children, which may lead to additional problems (Black et al., 1992). This negative affect can prompt the child to suppress his or her emotions and thereby inhibit "normal" grieving.

Additionally, if placed with relatives of the victim, the child may avoid talking about the murder due to fear of upsetting adults. Conversely, the adults may be too preoccupied with their own grieving processes to effectively facilitate the child's adaptive bereavement process (Black & Kaplan, 1988). Finally, some children may respond to this stressor by exhibiting regressive behavior. For example, enuresis has been observed in some children who experience the murder of one parent by the other (Black & Kaplan, 1988).

ELDER ABUSE

Following the identification of child abuse and spousal violence in our society, the elderly were the next group identified as being at risk of being targets of violence in the home (Pillemer & Finkelhor, 1989). However, knowledge about this area of family violence has been somewhat slow in developing (Beck & Ferguson, 1981) and most clinicians do not receive any kind of formal education in the identification or treatment of elder abuse (Tilden et al., 1994).

Four specific areas have been delineated in which the elderly may commonly experience abuse from family members: violation of rights, material abuse, physical abuse, and psychological abuse (Beck & Ferguson, 1981). Violation of rights consists of neglect such as not providing adequate food or medical care. Material abuse includes theft or misappropriation of funds, such as stealing an elderly person's Social Security check. Physical abuse comprises such acts as beatings and overmedicating the elderly. Finally, psychological abuse includes verbal threats and isolating the elderly person from others.

Thelma represents a fairly typical, but somewhat subtle, case of elder abuse. She was 71 years old when we treated her on an adult inpatient unit. She had been diagnosed with bipolar disorder 25 years earlier. She was placed on lithium at that time and took it regularly for many years. Thelma had recently moved in with her divorced daughter and 5-year-old grandson. Even though Thelma was having difficulty taking care of herself, her daughter expected Thelma to watch the grandson while she was at work as well as administer her own medication. Thelma was admitted to the unit after she ran out of her medication and started to exhibit symptoms of mania, including pressured speech. It quickly became clear to us that Thelma had memory problems and was not competent to care for herself, let alone a young child. Thelma's daughter did not visit her during her hospitalization. Additionally, her telephone was disconnected and Thelma was unable to remember where the daughter worked, so we were unable to contact the daughter for several weeks to collect additional information. In effect, Thelma had been abandoned by her daughter and we eventually had to place her in a nursing home.

The Prevalence and Etiology of Elder Abuse

It has been posited that elder abuse is relatively rare in some cultures, perhaps due to increased respect for elders as sources of wisdom (Kashani et al., 1992). However, Western society does not always uphold these ideals and may ignore or ridicule the older members of the family unit. Additionally, in Western culture, violence directed toward the elderly does not seem to be as taboo as child abuse (Johnson, 1979).

In a study of elder abuse in the general population, Pillemer and Finkelhor (1989) estimated that approximately 3.2% of elders are victims of violence within their homes. Additionally, as is typical with most forms of family violence, underreporting of elder abuse appears to be a problem (Johnson, 1979). In contrast to data on nonelderly adults, which indicate that women are at greater risk for abuse, elderly men and women appear to have similar rates of abuse (Pillemer & Finkelhor, 1989).

Among possible risk factors for violence against persons who are elderly, several authors (e.g., Johnson, 1979) have compared it with child abuse. Essentially, the elderly are sometimes incorrectly viewed as having "regressed" back to a dependent and childlike state (Beck & Ferguson, 1981; Johnson, 1979). Their frustration at being treated like children may cause them to act in a manner that is viewed by their younger caretakers as selfish or unacceptable and thus leads to tension in this relationship (Beck & Ferguson, 1981).

The etiologic model that has received the most attention in the literature involves the potential resentment, termed *caregiver stress,* developed by an adult child when having to care for a dependent parent (Kosberg, 1988; Pillemer & Finkelhor, 1989). For example, numerous hardships are created by having elderly parents residing with the family, including financial burdens, time pressures, and cramped housing (Johnson, 1979). This factor has been largely accepted as putting the elderly at risk, and it has been given a great deal of credence in the media and popular literature. However, empirical support is largely lacking for this theory.

In contrast, some initial empirical support has been gathered indicating that the more problematic issue may involve the dependence of the adult caregiver on his or her elder charge. It has been noted that in two thirds of reported cases of elder abuse, the adult child was financially dependent upon the elderly parent (see Pillemer & Finkelhor, 1989). Based on social exchange theory, it makes sense that violence toward the elder person could occur if the adult child experiences a perceived lack or loss of power and uses physical violence to help restore equilibrium (Pillemer & Finkelhor, 1989).

In fact, Pillemer and Finkelhor (1989), in one of the few studies to systematically examine possible etiologies of elder abuse, found that elder abuse is generally associated with the abuser's personality problems and dependency on the older person rather than any inherent stress on the adult child caregiver from having to care for dependent elderly parents. Thus the characteristics of the abuser seem to be more relevant to the topic than the characteristics of the elderly person who is abused. Additionally, the most frequent perpetrators of elder abuse are not grown children who are resentful for having to care for elder parents but, instead, are the elders' spouses (Pillemer & Finkelhor, 1989).

The intergenerational transmission theory discussed in Chapter 2 is also sometimes invoked for describing elder abuse (Griffin & Williams, 1992). Children who are abused by their parents therefore may be at risk for later abusing their parents when they become older and more susceptible. This pattern could be absorbed via social learning or could be an attempt of the adult child to get revenge on the parents for unresolved conflicts related to the abuse (Griffin & Williams, 1992).

The Impact of Elder Abuse on Children

In our 1992 review of the literature (Kashani et al., 1992), we noted that "thus far, the impact of elder abuse upon children who witness this violence is not well studied or documented" (p. 185). The same condition still exists and no new literature, to our knowledge, has appeared that addresses this potentially crucial problem. However, one likely outcome of a child witnessing elder abuse may be the child's confusion due to expectations that, because of their frailty as well as increased life experience, older people should be treated with respect and kindness (Kashani et al., 1992). At least we can anticipate or hypothesize that witnessing the abuse of another human being, especially an invalid or helpless person, might serve as a model for a young child and result in the child later directing violence toward others.

At this time, it is unknown whether this lack of research is due to difficulty in gathering an adequate sample or other unidentified factors. For example, researchers in gerontology may have little interest in the effects of elder abuse on children. However, as our population ages and people continue to live longer, growing cohabitation between children and grandparents seems likely to occur. Again, we will optimistically echo our earlier sentiment (Kashani et al., 1992) that future studies should investigate the putative effects (e.g., internalizing problems, dysfunctional attitudes) of elder abuse on children and the impact on the entire family system and environment.

SUMMARY

A number of studies have documented that externalizing, internalizing, and social problems frequently seem to develop in children and adolescents who witness violence in the home. However, many of these findings are obscured by the reliance on information pertaining to children and adolescents residing in battered women's shelters. Due to the strangeness of the situation to children, their behavior may be temporarily changed, and results reported in the literature as attributable to the impact of witnessing family violence may be at least partially ascribed to shelter status.

Many initial studies in this area lumped together youngsters of different ages (Fantuzzo et al., 1991). More recent research has examined separate cohorts and has found age to be an important determinant of the effects of family violence on children. Overall, young children seem to be the most studied and best understood population with regard to their reactions to witnessing family violence between parents. As children reach adolescence, their symptom constellations become more diverse and they are a more heterogenous group than younger children (McCloskey et al., 1995).

Gender does not seem to be a significant factor in the impact of witnessing spousal violence among preschoolers (Fantuzzo et al., 1991; Hughes & Barad, 1983). In contrast, gender differences emerge as children get older and males tend to display more externalizing symptoms in particular (e.g., Porter & O'Leary, 1980). Females seem to cope generally better than males after observing marital violence.

In general, because studies have identified such a wide variety of symptoms that may be exhibited by children and adolescents who witness violence, a clear reaction pattern has not surfaced. Nevertheless, we can say with confidence that witnessing violence in the home has clear untoward effects on children and adolescents that may be manifested in a variety of ways.

5

PSYCHOLOGICAL MALTREATMENT WITHIN THE FAMILY

We all remember the childhood taunt, "Sticks and stones will break my bone, but words will never hurt me." Researchers and clinicians are likely to strongly disagree with this sentiment, particularly when it is applied in cases of family maltreatment. In contrast to physical violence within the family, emotional or psychological abuse that is perpetrated by one family member on another has received relatively little attention, which is unfortunate given the adverse effects such abuse can have on children.

One reason for this situation may be the somewhat amorphous nature of this type of familial violence as well as the variety of labels that are used to describe it. Some authors, for example, prefer the term *emotional abuse* whereas others select the phrase *psychological abuse*. Perhaps the most useful and all-encompassing nomenclature is *psychological maltreatment* (Edmundson & Collier, 1993).

Psychological maltreatment is the "denial of essential psychological nutrients or the denigration of personal worth through domination techniques and patterns of interaction which are damaging to the emerging personality" (Nesbit & Karagianis, 1987, p. 180). It sometimes accompanies physical familial violence as well as sexual abuse and neglect, but it can also occur alone. We agree that *psychological maltreatment* is probably the most accurate and functional expression and will use this phrase most frequently.

Psychological maltreatment can include parent-to-parent abuse that is observed by the child as well as parent-to-child behaviors. This conduct includes such parental behaviors as threatening, rejecting, isolating, ignoring, yelling, labeling, humiliating, scapegoating, name-calling, giving excessive responsibilities, and withholding affection (Nesbit & Karagianis, 1987). Scapegoating, in particular, seems to be a common form of family violence (Nesbit & Karagianis, 1987) and one we discuss further in Chapter 2.

Another reason that psychological maltreatment may be less well documented than physical family violence is the fact that the presence of psychological maltreatment is hard to prove in the legal system (Yates, 1982) and may be downplayed by law officials. Can you imagine the response that would be given to a child who calls "911" because his or her parents called him or her a dirty name? In addition, there is an erroneous belief that overt types of abuse (e.g., hitting, kicking) exert more severe effects on children and adolescents than psychological abuse. True, physical violence can result in immediate tissue and other bodily damage, including broken bones, head injury, and even death. Even though the impact of psychological maltreatment may not be as conspicuous or immediate as physical violence, the insidious impact it can have on children and adolescents is notable and potentially severe. In fact, adolescents who have experienced physical and psychological maltreatment by a family member will sometimes report that they were bothered more by the emotional violence than by the physical trauma (Jurich, 1990). Nevertheless, this type of family violence usually must reach extreme levels before it is recognized as psychopathological by family members, mental health professionals, or others.

ETIOLOGY AND PREVALENCE OF PSYCHOLOGICAL MALTREATMENT

Marital separation has been cited as a major etiologic variable associated with emotional abuse (Preston, 1986), particularly between spouses. However, general family breakdown appears to be another major factor in the emergence of this family violence (Preston, 1986), perhaps because of the stress these occurrences place on the family unit. In terms of prevalence, some authors (e.g., O'Leary & Jouriles, 1994) have suggested that nearly every adult commits some kind of psychological maltreatment, of either a child or an adult partner. However, the frequency, content, and intensity of this violence can vary widely and determine the consequent effects (O'Leary & Jouriles, 1994).

In terms of frequency, infrequent spousal psychological maltreatment that is witnessed by a child does not seem to exert much impact on that child (O'Leary & Jouriles, 1994). Regarding content, parental disagreements regarding the child that are observed by that child seem to have the largest influence on child functioning (O'Leary & Jouriles, 1994). These disagreements may commonly center on issues of child-rearing practice. Intensity, however, is a more complex matter as most studies tend to operationalize psychological maltreatment as a less intense form of family violence, with physical and sexual abuse being higher on the hierarchy (O'Leary & Jouriles, 1994). Thus we do not know much about intense psychological maltreatment versus a less intense form of this violence.

IMPACT OF PSYCHOLOGICAL MALTREATMENT ON CHILDREN AND ADOLESCENTS

The child variable that has been examined most frequently in relation to psychological maltreatment is attachment to significant others. Secure attachment to parental figures has been posited as a necessary step for a child in developing competence and adequate functioning. Parental rejection, in particular, seems to disrupt the attachment process and lead to insecure attachment (Wright, 1994). This pattern of attachment, first established with parents, seems to be repeated with other persons throughout the child's lifetime. Thus a child who is insecurely attached to his or her parents seems to have interpersonal problems that are ongoing and pervasive.

Some children who experience psychological maltreatment may externalize their pain and act out as a form of coping. We treated Patrick, a 12-year-old male, for behavioral problems in an outpatient clinic. Patrick's family life had been chaotic and he was psychologically abused by many family members. His parents had difficulties with substance abuse and had not bonded with or adequately cared for Patrick. When Patrick was 6 years old, he went to live with his grandmother, who was a caring person but was overwhelmed by having to raise a young child at her age. His parents would occasionally call Patrick and promise to visit him. A date would be set and Patrick would become excited by the prospect of seeing them. However, they invariably would not show up or call. The incidents would be followed by his grandmother criticizing Patrick's parents in front of him, calling them "potheads," and telling Patrick that he was a fool for believing that his parents would come for a visit. This pattern continued for several years until we saw the family. At that time, the psychological maltreatment had increased and the grandmother frequently disparaged Patrick by calling him "lazy" and "stupid." To address this problem, indirect methods were used with the grandmother, such as encouraging her to spend positive time with Patrick. However, she became angry and pointed out to us that Patrick had the problem, not her. Not surprisingly, Patrick had little motivation for treatment and the family dropped out prematurely.

Our own work (Allan, Kashani, & Reid, in press) with inpatient children has documented that self-reported parental hostility is associated with the simultaneous presence of familial problems. For example, families with a hostile parent tend to have little cohesion or emotional bonding, warmth, and concern for the child's well-being. Perhaps as a result, the children in these families tend to have poor social skills and are described by their parents as more socially incompetent than children who do not have hostile parents. Even less work has examined the impact on child witnessing of verbal violence between parents. Fantuzzo and colleagues (1991), however, did find that parental verbal violence alone was related to moderate problems with children's conduct, but not to emotional or internalizing problems. Beatrice, for example, witnessed tremendous verbal struggles between her parents when she was young. Her mother was an intelligent person, although she was not warm or affectionate. Her father was also very bright, but he tended to be extremely angry and critical. He would frequently make fun of others and had a hard time keeping a job. At times, the parents would argue and the father would threaten to kill Beatrice's younger brother Ralph. Beatrice often overheard these tirades. As Beatrice grew, she began to experience problems with anger control, feelings of worthlessness, and extreme interpersonal oversensitivity.

SUMMARY

Because of the lack of overt physical abuse in families where psychological maltreatment is present, this form of family violence may be overlooked by mental health professionals, teachers, and other adults as well as the family members themselves. Only when the maltreatment becomes severe and obvious may steps be taken to remediate this problem.

Although we are beginning to understand psychological maltreatment and the ways it can affect children who witness it between spouses or experience it from a parent, many other aspects of psychological maltreatment have not yet been examined and await empirical documentation. For example, sibling-on-sibling emotional abuse, such as name-calling, is fairly routine in our society. This problem may be given a relatively high degree of parental tolerance and may affect children in various and potentially serious ways.

Years of working with families have led us to form the opinion that psychological maltreatment is an even more important health issue for children and adolescents than physical abuse and can be more damaging; others seem to agree (e.g., Nesbit & Karagianis, 1987). As we discuss in the final chapter, this area of family violence seems to be the unexplored and next frontier in the burgeoning literature on family violence.

6

CROSS-CULTURAL PERSPECTIVE

PATTERNS OF VIOLENCE
IN OTHER CULTURES

As we have discussed previously, family violence occurs in all types of American households. Violence, outside of and within the family unit, is widespread and endemic. When examining proposed etiologies of family violence in Chapter 2, we touched upon the fact that some theories of family violence indicate that social and ecological factors may play a role in the genesis and maintenance of violence. Questions then arise about the frequency and nature of family violence in other societies. Perhaps families in other societies may commonly possess risk or protective factors that increase or decrease the probability of family violence.

Different societies tend to have disparate types of family constellations (Levinson, 1989). These subtypes typically include the nuclear family composed of two parents and their children, the matrifocal family consisting of the mother and her children, the polygynous family with a father and his wives and children, and the extended family encompassing any number of relatives (Levinson, 1989). As the number of people in a family increases, the number of possible unique relationships increases as well. So, in a matrifocal family with one child, there is only one relationship, mother-child. In large extended families, there are a multitude of relationships, including spousal, mother-child, father-child, sibling, child-grandparent, cousins, and so forth. Given the vast differences, both practical and logistical, between these types of families, it seems intuitive that family violence could vary accordingly.

Although family violence has received a great deal of recent attention in the United States, many countries, particularly nonindustrialized ones, have not yet given this topic the same amount of consideration or recognition. Cases of family violence may go overlooked in other cultures. Osuna and colleagues (1995), for instance, found that fewer than 10% of "highly probable" cases of family violence examined in a medical setting in Spain were so identified. In 1980, however, the United Nations, recognizing the insidious nature of family violence, held the Conference on Equality, Development, and Peace (Reichert, 1991) and implored member nations to ratify resolutions to defend victims of family violence as well as mobilize intervention and prevention programs.

However, as a result of the current lag, hard empirical data concerning family violence in other societies are sparse and overreliant on case studies and anthropological fieldwork. These data may not be as useful overall as the carefully designed studies being conducted in Western countries; however, it is anticipated that the data may provide some insight into the nature of human aggression.

Initially, many authors theorized that the lack of documentation of family violence in certain cultures most likely indicated that it was not routine in these societies. Some authors even conjectured that, instead of being a universal trait of human nature, family violence may be concurrent with and inseparable from the many other problems manifest in Western society (Korbin, 1995). Garbarino (1977), for example, cites the privacy and isolation of the nuclear family in Western society as a main reason that family violence can occur in the United States and continue without abatement.

Often the old adage, "It takes a village to raise a child," is invoked as a likely explanation regarding the possible absence of family violence in some preindustrial societies. However, Korbin (1995) points out that this statement assumes that people in small-scale societies look out for and protect children, even children who are not their own biological relatives. Available data suggest that this simply does not occur. Just as family violence was once hidden in the United States, health care professionals in other societies are beginning to see the emergence of family violence. No doubt, to assume that family violence does not occur simply because it is not openly discussed in a society constitutes a case of faulty reasoning (Reichert, 1991).

Even within a society like the United States where abuse is given a great deal of attention, complications ensue when attempting to compare rates of abuse from state to state due to differences in reporting laws and community standards (Korbin, 1995). As can be imagined, comparing family violence across societies is difficult due to differing opinions of what constitutes abuse. Additionally, some countries do not have reporting systems that are analogous to those systems found in Western societies (Korbin, 1995). Thus cross-cultural comparisons are difficult and fraught with methodological problems but may be helpful in gaining additional insight into the nature of intrafamilial aggression. We will begin by reviewing available data concerning the victims of family violence and then will examine what it means to be a "culture without violence."

SPOUSAL VIOLENCE

As in Western societies, spousal violence cross-culturally most frequently involves husbands beating their wives (Korbin, 1995). This type of violence occurs at least some of the time and is reported in approximately 84.5% of societies (Levinson, 1989). Husband abuse is also reported in about 26.9% of societies (Levinson, 1989). Conspicuously, however, husband abuse only transpires in societies in which wife beating is also observed. Violence toward wives also seems to occur most often in societies where women are ranked below men in status. The presence of polygynous families (i.e., one male and multiple females) in other cultures allows an interesting comparison for family violence. According to Levinson (1989), physical violence between women happens almost prohibitively in cultures with polygynous marriages. Notably, in polygynous families, woman-to-woman violence often concerns arguments over sexual access to the husband.

VIOLENCE TOWARD CHILDREN

It is surprising how little work has examined the frequency or nature of violence toward children in other societies, perhaps because it is a relatively taboo topic and is a low base-rate event, even in most families that are violent (Levinson, 1989). However, this lack of reporting may be due somewhat to reporter bias. Korbin (1995) notes that, in his work concerning rural Hawaiian, Polynesian Americans, he occasionally observed child abuse. However, because it was so aberrant from the cultural pattern of child care, which typically involves a great deal of love and attention, he did not make reports of it in the literature for many years. Thus this population was largely considered violence-free prior to his later reports.

Cross-cultural work indicates that it is uncommon for infants to be the target of intrafamilial violence (Levinson, 1989). However, infanticide, although rare overall, is found in many different cultures (Levinson, 1989). Severe violence directed toward children also is unusual (Levinson, 1989). In the United States, the form of family violence most frequently seen is sibling violence (Korbin, 1995). Cross-culturally, the primary type of family violence exerted on children is physical punishment that is overly punitive.

Another area of abuse involves initiation ceremonies that mark an adolescent's transition from childhood to young adulthood. These ceremonies include operations on the genitals, tattooing, and forced starvation (Levinson, 1989). Although many people argue that these ceremonies should not be considered abuse because everybody in the culture is expected to endure the same initiation, Levinson (1989) for one disagrees. He notes that the pain inflicted during such ceremonies is sanctioned by the parents and conducted by people known to the family, and thus constitutes family violence.

VIOLENCE TOWARD ELDERS

A myth exists that the elderly are venerated in many societies, particularly peasant and other small-scale cultures, and are not victims of violence or abuse (Korbin, 1995). Conversely, in some societies, the elderly may be left behind or forced to commit suicide when they grow too old to contribute to the group. However, this practice seems to be isolated to a few nomadic tribes and typically only occurs when the elderly person is too ill or frail to continue to travel with the group (Levinson, 1989). Overall, the treatment afforded the elderly seems to diverge rather dramatically from culture to culture based largely on the beliefs and attitudes of the society.

PERCEIVED EFFECTS
OF FAMILY VIOLENCE

Although the effects of family violence on its victims are well documented in Western society, peoples in other societies may not be aware of the relationship between aggression and mental health problems in family members. This assertion is supplied with preliminary documentation by Reichert (1991), who surveyed international students at an American university. Students from industrialized countries were more aware than students from Third World societies of the negative impact family abuse can have on children and other family members.

Family violence, from place to place, does appear to vary in terms of type, frequency, and cause (Levinson, 1989). Overall, we have to agree with Levinson's (1989) assertion that "most people in the world have at some time been either the perpetrator of, the victim of, or a witness to violence between family members" (p. 9).

SOCIETIES WITHOUT VIOLENCE

Although data suggest that family violence is exceedingly common throughout cultures, a few societies seem to have such low rates of intrafamilial aggression that calling them "societies without violence" is appropriate (Korbin, 1995). Levinson (1989), in the largest cross-cultural study of family violence to date, delineated 16 such small-scale societies that are distributed throughout the seven continents. Included in this tally are the South American Ona and Pemon, the Bushmen of Africa, the Asian Central Thai and Andamans, and the Iroquois of North America. In terms of economic systems, these societies differ widely between hunter-gatherers, horticulturists, agriculturists, and herders. However, notably, hunter-gatherer societies were overrepresented, perhaps because of the importance of having every family member participate in the acquisition of food.

Based on studies of these 16 societies, Levinson (1989) forwarded some preliminary observations concerning commonalities between these violence-free cultures. Husbands and wives tend to share in household decision making and the wives also profit from the product of family work. In terms of marriage, it is monogamous, and divorce is not common. However, wives can initiate divorce as easily as husbands. During the marriage, husbands and wives sleep together in the same room and, prior to marriage, a sexual double standard does not exist in relation to premarital sexual activity. Disputes between men are solved peacefully and without aggression. Finally, intervention for spousal abuse (i.e., wife beating) characteristically occurs without delay.

These factors focus exclusively on relationships between spouses, which is typical of the cross-cultural family violence literature as it highlights spouse abuse, perhaps because it is more easily measured or less hidden than child abuse. However, a good spousal relationship is an important foundation for a healthy family and many lessons can be learned from these societies. Korbin (1995) adds a strong social network as a factor that can help limit the extent of family violence. Such a network provides boundaries concerning the nature of acceptable violence as well as promoting a couple's resolution of a dispute.

In conclusion, societies that are comparably free from family violence seem to emphasize cooperation, commitment, sharing, and equality between members. These qualities will be discussed again in Chapter 9 when prevention is considered. As indicated by Levinson (1989), *"the absence of family violence in some societies . . . provide[s] proof that family violence is neither 'natural' nor uncontrollable"* (p. 24).

SUMMARY

Despite differing attitudes and beliefs from culture to culture, family violence appears to be an omnipresent force throughout the world. Spouses, children, and the elderly are abused or witness violence toward others. Initial reports that family violence was unique to industrialized societies are grossly overstated and may instead reflect a lack of awareness in nonindustrialized countries regarding identification of familial aggression. Of note, however, there are a few small-scale communities that have very low rates of family violence, and they may shed light on ways to prevent violence.

7

ASSESSMENT STRATEGIES

Mental health professionals are often called upon to evaluate children who have been abused or who have vicariously observed violence in the home. Thus knowledge of pertinent assessment techniques is important. This chapter will commence with some general methods that will facilitate child assessment in these types of cases. From there, assessment issues pertaining to the degree of child abuse, degree of child witnessing of family violence, impact of family violence on the child, and familial functioning will be considered.

GENERAL CHILD ASSESSMENT

During the assessment procedure, rapport needs to be built with the child. Violence issues are an extremely sensitive area and it will likely be difficult for a child or adolescent to discuss these topics with a new or unfamiliar person. Therefore, the initial goal is to get to know the child. Clinicians may wish to begin by talking about nonabuse issues. For younger children, the mental health professional may ask them about the clothes they are wearing, their favorite television shows, their friends, or a variety of other relatively neutral subjects. Playing ball with them for a few minutes can also help break the ice and create a more relaxed atmosphere. To assess their ability to answer questions in a realistic and accurate manner, the child can be asked to describe different colors of crayons and the gender of dolls. We also like to show them pictures of "mad," "sad," and "happy" faces and have them report about these emotions to informally assess their ability to report on affect. For older children and adolescents, asking them about school, friends, interests, or hobbies can help them feel comfortable.

The majority of clinicians do not systematically assess for family violence when seeing children or their families (Tilden et al., 1994). However, assessment is imperative for the mental health or other professional who is working with children from violent families. Before treatment can begin, a careful assessment should be conducted. Treatment should be assessment driven; protocols or components are selected based upon the findings of the assessment.

ASSESSMENT OF DEGREE
OF CHILD ABUSE

The primary mode of gathering information regarding the extent of violence experienced by a child is the unstructured or semistructured interview. Additionally, a few structured interviews contain sections on abuse, although they tend to focus on sexual abuse. Clinicians who encounter child abuse may therefore need to develop their own protocols. A number of issues should be discussed, perhaps focusing on the nature, severity, and extent of abuse suffered or witnessed by a child. Additionally, the number and relationships of the perpetrator(s) to the child are important.

Standardized assessment of the degree of child abuse or maltreatment has not received a great deal of attention in the literature. However, one questionnaire has recently been validated to assess this area. The Childhood Trauma Questionnaire (CTQ; Bernstein, Ahluvalia, Pogge, & Handelsman, 1997) is a 70-item measure that evaluates reports of abuse by children and adolescents. A factor analysis has revealed five components of the scale: emotional abuse, emotional neglect, sexual abuse, physical abuse, and physical neglect. Thus the CTQ assesses a broad range of abusive and neglectful behaviors directed toward children and adolescents.

Although this scale clearly represents a step in the right direction, it should be noted that questions request that respondents report their "experiences growing up." Thus it does not differentiate between past and present abuse and does not provide information concerning when particular events may have occurred. Additionally, the scale has only been validated for adolescents in an inpatient population, and the potential usefulness of the scale with children and nonhospitalized adolescents is not yet established.

ASSESSMENT OF DEGREE OF
CHILD WITNESSING OF FAMILY VIOLENCE

One of the most ignored areas of family violence has been the assessment of child witnessing of intrafamilial brutality. However, increased awareness of the negative impact such witnessing can have on children has been accompanied by the appearance of assessment strategies. As with child abuse, the principal assessment tool is the personal unstructured or semistructured interview.

The O'Leary-Porter Scale (OPS; Porter & O'Leary, 1980) is a 20-item inventory that assesses the frequency of conflict between parents that occurs in front of the child. Specific questions evaluate how often different forms of dissension, such as verbal arguments, sarcasm, or violence, are observed by a child. Another questionnaire has been developed more recently, the Child Witness to Violence Interview (Jaffe, Wilson, & Wolfe, 1989). This scale comprises 42 items and assesses three domains germane to children who have witnessed family violence. First, the child's attitudes and beliefs about anger are explored. This section includes questions regarding the degree to which a child views violence as a suitable means to resolve conflict. Second, a child's safety skills are examined and include a child's knowledge about how to keep him- or herself safe during episodes of intrafamilial violence. Third, the child's tendency to ascribe blame for family violence to him- or herself is assessed.

ASSESSMENT OF THE IMPACT
OF FAMILY VIOLENCE ON THE CHILD

Assessment of the child's functioning often begins via a semistructured interview regarding his or her perceptions of, understanding of, and feelings regarding the violence (Wolfe & Bourdeau, 1987). To measure overall, or global, child functioning, the Children's Global Assessment Scale (CGAS; Shaffer et al., 1983) may be considered. The scale, which can be used for children ages 4 to 16 years old, provides a "single, unidimensional, global measure of severity of disturbance and adequacy of social function" (Shaffer et al., 1983, p. 1228). Thus it permits an assessor (i.e., a clinician or researcher) to integrate information about diverse aspects of a particular child's functioning and consolidate these data into a discrete index of level of well-being (Shaffer et al., 1983). Scores range from 1, which exemplifies the most disturbed child, to 100, which illustrates superior functioning (Shaffer et al., 1983). Normal functioning is indicated by scores greater than 70 (Shaffer et al., 1983), as documented by Bird and colleagues (1990).

As we have discussed in earlier chapters, four primary areas of child functioning are commonly affected by the presence of family violence: externalizing symptoms, internalizing symptoms, cognitive functioning, and social functioning. Frequently used measures in these domains will be discussed below.

Externalizing Symptoms

Several measures have been developed to assess a child's externalizing behaviors. Additionally, these questionnaires typically have parallel forms that elicit information from youths, parents, and teachers. Some of the most commonly used measures in this category include the Conners Parent's Rating scale (Conners, 1985) and the Behavior Problem Checklist (Quay & Peterson, 1975).

One of the primary measures used to assess children's externalizing behavior is the Child Behavior Checklist, which was developed by Achenbach (1991). It is a broad-band measure and includes scales for externalizing and internalizing behaviors. Separate forms exist for parent, teacher, and youth self-report. The scale consists of 113 items that are rated on a 0 (not true) to 2 (very true or often true) scale. Good reliability and validity have been found for the scale (Achenbach, 1991), and it is one of the most extensively used child assessment measures.

In addition to questionnaire data, a structured or semistructured interview also may be of use. These interviews include the Diagnostic Interview for Children and Adolescents (DICA; Herjanic & Reich, 1982), the Schedule for Affective Disorders and Schizophrenia for School-Age Children (K-SADS; Chambers et al., 1985), and the Diagnostic Interview Schedule for Children and Adolescents (DISC; Costello, Edelbrock, & Costello, 1985). Mental health professionals should give particular attention to diagnoses such as conduct disorder and substance use/abuse for children and adolescents who have experienced family violence.

Internalizing Symptoms

Internalizing symptoms in the form of anxiety and depression are frequently displayed by children from violent families. Fortunately, a variety of useful assessment tools have been developed to evaluate internalizing symptoms in children, including interviews and questionnaires.

Structured interviews. The interviews reviewed in the previous section on externalizing problems are also applicable for assessing internalizing disorders/symptoms. One particularly useful interview for this population is the Anxiety Disorders Interview Schedule for Children (ADIS-C) and its parallel parent version (ADIS-P) (Silverman & Nelles, 1988). The ADIS-C and the ADIS-P were developed to provide differential diagnoses of childhood disorders, with a particular focus on internalizing disorders. Both interviews have been found to be reliable and valid for use with children and adolescents

(Silverman & Eisen, 1992) and to assess for a wide variety of child and adolescent disorders, including separation anxiety disorder, major depression, panic disorder, agoraphobia, post-traumatic stress disorder, affective disorders, attention deficit hyperactivity disorder, and substance abuse.

Questionnaires. When completing self-report questionnaires, some children who have experienced family violence may distort their responses to maintain social desirability (Wolfe & Bourdeau, 1987). Despite this potential problem, many useful questionnaires have been developed to evaluate internalizing symptoms in children and adolescents. These measures are broken into three primary groups: anxiety, depression, and other internalizing measures.

The Revised Children's Manifest Anxiety Scale (RCMAS; Reynolds & Richmond, 1978) is a 37-item yes-no instrument that assesses three anxiety factors: (a) physiological, (b) worry/oversensitivity, and (c) concentration (Reynolds & Paget, 1981). Additionally, it has a lie scale that may help identify cases where social desirability may be problematic. The RCMAS is the most widely used child anxiety measure; however, it has been criticized for including many items that overlap with other disorders, such as ADHD and depression (Perrin & Last, 1992).

To help remediate this problem, March, Parker, Sullivan, Stallings, and Conners (1997) developed the Multidimensional Anxiety Scale for Children (MASC). The MASC contains four factors: physical symptoms, harm avoidance, social anxiety, and separation anxiety, and shows initial promise as a measure of child anxiety. In fact, several major research programs, such as the University of Chicago, have already adopted the MASC for studies (M. Reinecke, personal communication, April 11, 1997).

Other anxiety scales include the State-Trait Anxiety Inventory for Children (STAIC; Spielberger, 1973), which contains two anxiety subscales. The A-State form (STAIC-S) consists of 20 statements that ask the child how he or she feels at a particular moment, whereas the A-Trait form (STAIC-T) contains items that assess how the child generally feels. For each item, the stem phrase "I feel" is provided and the child chooses from one of three adjectives furnished. The Revised Fear Survey Schedule for Children (FSSC-R; Ollendick, 1983) is an 80-item scale of general fearfulness in youngsters. The FSSC-R assesses number, severity, and types of fears, many of which may be displayed by children from violent families.

The Children's Depression Inventory (CDI; Kovacs, 1992) is a 27-item measure of childhood depression. Each item of the scale is composed of three statements, and the child circles the statement that he or she thinks best describes him or her within the last two weeks. Each item is then scored from

0 to 2 points with a total possible score ranging from 0 to 54 points, with 19 and above indicating clinical depression. The Children's Depression Rating scale is a 17-item clinician rating scale that was developed by Poznanski, Cook, and Carroll (1979) to assess the level of depressive symptomatology in children and adolescents.

The Scale for Suicide Ideation (Beck, Kovacs, & Weissman, 1979) was developed to quantify and assess the degree of suicidal ideation in adults. It is a clinician rating scale that is completed following a semistructured interview with the child or adolescent (Schotte & Clum, 1982). The clinician or other mental health professional evaluates 19 items that assess three broad dimensions of suicidal ideation: active suicidal desire, suicide plans, and passive suicidal desire (Beck, Kovacs, & Weissman, 1979). Possible scores range from 0 to 38, and higher scores are indicative of greater levels of suicidal ideation. This clinician rating scale has been validated for use with adolescents (Steer, Kumar, & Beck, 1993) and, recently, for children (Allan, Kashani, Dahlmeier, Taghizadeh, & Reid, in press). The Hopelessness Scale for Children was developed by Kazdin and colleagues (1983) for children ages 6 to 13 years old and was patterned after the adult Hopelessness Scale (Beck, Weissman, Lester, & Trexler, 1974). The scale consists of 17 items that are rated as "true" or "false" by a child. Total scores, ranging from 0 to 17, are computed by adding the score for each item. Higher scores signify elevated hopelessness or pessimistic expectations of the future (Kazdin, Rodgers, & Colbus, 1986). Although designed for children, the scale was used successfully with 17-year-olds by Kashani, Reid, and Rosenberg (1989).

Cognitive Functioning

The most widely used measures for cognitive functioning are the Wechsler scales. The Wechsler Preschool and Primary Scale of Intelligence (WPPSI; Wechsler, 1967) can be used for children ages 4 through 6 years of age. For older children (6 to 16 years old), the Wechsler Intelligence Scale for Children (WISC-III; Wechsler, 1991) is useful. Both of these tests are divided into performance and verbal components and also provide a full scale IQ score. These tests are frequently used by school districts throughout the United States, which increases the likelihood that the child has been tested with one or both previously and therefore has prior scores for comparison with current functioning. Other frequently used cognitive measures include the Stanford-Binet Intelligence Scale (Thorndike, Hagen, & Sattler, 1986) and the Kaufman Assessment Battery for Children (K-ABC; Kaufman & Kaufman, 1983).

Social Functioning

Perhaps the most widely used social competence scale is the CBCL (Achenbach, 1991), which includes a section assessing the child's activities, social participation, and school performance. In terms of assessing social skills, the Matson Evaluation of Social Skills (MESSY; Matson, 1990) provides in-depth data regarding a child's performance of specific appropriate (e.g., helping a friend) and inappropriate (e.g., bragging) social behaviors. The MESSY has a self-report and teacher/parent report form and has been found to be related to a variety of markers of social functioning (Bell-Dolan & Allan, 1997; Matson, 1990).

FAMILY ASSESSMENT

Family assessment for violent families is based on the tenet that the family is an "interactional system in which each member contributes to the dysfunctional climate" (Wolfe & Bourdeau, 1987, p. 277). This type of assessment becomes most important in cases where the child or adolescent is to be maintained in or returned to the family where violence has occurred. Although prediction of violence is not possible, the mental health professional can assess the quality of the home environment, which can also be crucial. Behavioral observation during therapy sessions and perhaps within the home can help provide much of this information.

Another area that can be assessed is the manner in which conflicts between parents and children are resolved. The Conflicts Tactic Scale (Straus, 1979), for example, assesses the manner in which family members address interpersonal conflict. Three modes of conflict resolution are evaluated: verbal reasoning, verbal aggression, and physical aggression. This scale appears to be particularly useful in the assessment of the violent family (Wissow, Wilson, Roter, Larson, & Berman, 1992).

Another questionnaire that is frequently used is the Family Environment Scale (FES; Moos & Moos, 1984), which measures dimensions of family relationships. The FES is a 90-item scale that has analogous parent and child rating forms. Ten factors of family functioning are assessed: cohesion, expressiveness, conflict, independence, achievement, orientation, intellectual-cultural orientation, active-recreational orientation, moral-religious emphasis, organization, and control. Additionally, a discrepancy score can be computed to determine interrater agreement, such as agreement between child and parent. The scale is reliable and valid with good test-retest reliability and internal consistency. Glaser, Sayger, and Horne (1993) compared, via the

FES, families that were functional, distressed, or child abusive. Abusive families were characterized by high scores on the conflict and low scores on the expressiveness subscales of the FES when compared with the other types of families.

The Family Adaptability and Cohesion Scale III (Olson, 1986) is a 20-item instrument that evaluates two dimensions of family functioning: cohesion and adaptability. *Cohesion* is defined as the emotional bonding and individual autonomy of family members, and *adaptability* is defined as the family's ability to change its relationship rules, role relations, and power structure in response to situational and developmental stress (Olson, Russell, & Sprenkle, 1983). The questionnaire can be completed, using a five-point rating scale, by any member of a family. Good reliability (Olson, 1986) and validity (Edman, Cole, & Howard, 1990) have been established for the FACES-III.

A WORD ON VALIDATION
OF FAMILY VIOLENCE

The main focus of this book is on the psychological impact that familial violence often has on children and adolescents. Thus a full discussion of the validation of violence is beyond the scope of this book. We start with the assumption that abuse has already been validated. Fortunately, a plethora of articles and books have been written to address the topic of validation of child abuse. Although mental health professionals are mandated by law to report *any* suspected child abuse, in terms of actual effects and treatment needs, we are most concerned with *chronic* abuse.

The primary assessment tool in mental health for helping to validate child abuse is the semistructured or unstructured interview. A specific structured interview for assessing child abuse has not appeared in the literature. Therefore, mental health professionals may need to develop their own questions for such situations. The American Academy of Child and Adolescent Psychiatry (AACAP, 1997) recently developed and published their recommendations for this assessment. Most important, the clinician needs to clearly define his or her role as one of the following: forensic evaluator, clinician who will provide treatment, or consultant. In each of these roles, a mental health professional may be called upon for information from parents, legal authorities, or the court. Thus role definition will help determine the logical course of the assessment and subsequent activities.

SUMMARY

The assessment of family violence can take many forms. For child victims or witnesses of violence, assessing the degree of abuse experienced or witnessed may be fruitful. Additionally, the mental health professional has a variety of tools available to evaluate the possible psychological impact that family violence has had on a particular child. These tools include structured and semistructured interviews that provide diagnostic information and questionnaires that supply data on the child's functioning and levels of behavioral problems, anxiety, depression, and so forth. Use of these assessment methods allows a mental health professional to determine which areas of child functioning have been impaired by family violence and can help aid in the selection of relevant treatment targets.

Of note is the lack of instruments to document psychological abuse. Because chronic psychological abuse may be more damaging for a child than mild or transient physical abuse (see Chapter 5), there is great need for psychometrically sound measures to assess this important construct.

One critique of the literature in this area concerns overreliance on broad-band measures, such as the CBCL, as a tool to assess externalizing and internalizing problems as well as social competence. The CBCL is the most commonly used measure across all areas of child research; however, the use of more specific measures of externalizing and internalizing behaviors may be helpful. Future research could benefit from inclusion of other, more specific narrow-band instruments. For example, within the internalizing domain, use of the Children's Depression Inventory (Kovacs, 1992) and the Children's Manifest Anxiety Scale-Revised (Reynolds & Paget, 1983) may provide more detailed information about the unique constellation of symptoms displayed by children and adolescents.

8

INTERVENTION STRATEGIES FOR THE VIOLENT FAMILY

As is the case for several other familial problems, the violent family is unlikely to present for treatment and directly state the "true" complaint (Hurley & Jaffe, 1990; Jurich, 1990). Instead, the parents may focus on the child's oppositional conduct, deficient school performance, running away behavior, or poor peer relations. Therefore, the clinician must carefully evaluate the point of the system at which to intervene. Regardless of the target for intervention, the clinician should be aware that all family members will probably have some role in treatment and thus rapport and trust should be developed with each family member (Jurich, 1990).

Mandatory child abuse reporting laws now exist in every state (Brosig & Kalichman, 1992). If violence is suspected and has not yet come to the attention of the authorities, the clinician would benefit from letting the family know that child maltreatment will have to be reported. In this manner, the family members will be informed up front and will not feel betrayed by the therapist if he or she has to hotline the case, and the therapeutic relationship can remain intact. This goal is important as establishing and maintaining a "lifeline" between the therapist and the violent family can be crucial (Ryan, 1995). Ideally, the therapist can persuade the parent(s) to report the abuse themselves (Jurich, 1990), which can help increase their sense of self-control.

As in other chapters of this book where we have broken the impact of family violence into multiple sections (e.g., witnessing versus experiencing abuse), this chapter on treatment will consist of several different parts. Five general areas will be discussed that correspond to the target of the intervention: legal responses, treatment of the perpetrator of family violence, treatment of the child who has been abused, treatment of the child who has witnessed violence in the home, and treatment of the family that has experienced violence.

LEGAL RESPONSES

Historically, family violence was not illegal and was considered a private matter (Radbill, 1974). Today, child abuse is clearly unlawful and all mental health professionals are mandated to report suspected violence toward children (Brosig & Kalichman, 1992). Legal responses to child abuse are generally swift and include arrest and incarceration of offenders. In contrast, the response to spousal violence is often more variable. Although spousal violence is also illegal, mandated reporting does not exist except in cases of "imminent danger," which is somewhat ill-defined.

The police officer is generally the first legal authority with whom the abused spouse has contact. Often, when police officers are called to the scene of domestic violence, they may attempt to mediate between the partners rather than making an arrest (Home, 1991-1992). However, an arrest is more likely if the spouse has been physically injured by the violence (Bachman & Coker, 1995). Local police departments have received tremendous pressure to treat spousal violence with the same degree of urgency as violence between nonfamily members (Syers & Edelson, 1992).

Training programs now are provided to many police officers, and they are encouraged to supply information to spousal victims regarding emergency housing, legal counsel, and financial help (Home, 1991-1992). Many women's shelters, for example, provide legal advocacy to women who have been the targets of violence by mates (Edelson & Frank, 1991). Additionally, the courts have started to crack down on abusers, who often receive prison time. Violent offenders are often mandated into therapy or may be required to attend self-help groups, such as Parents Anonymous (Gelles & Maynard, 1987).

Often, family violence results in divorce or a relationship breakup. Due to the prevalence of bitter disputes between partners regarding issues such as custody and visitation, professionals have sought a less contentious solution—ediation. The main goal of this process is assisting the partners in amicably solving their disputes via conflict resolution and increased communication that is facilitated by a court-appointed mediator (Miller & Veltkamp, 1995).

Persons who have used mediation report satisfaction with the agreements devised as well as a sense of increased control over the process (Thoennes, Salem, & Pearson, 1995). Of note, mediation does tend to result in joint custody for the majority of cases and thus could be dangerous for some children in families with severe violence (Thoennes et al., 1995). However, about 70% of mediating agencies report that mediators receive some kind of specialized training related to domestic violence and 70% of agencies conduct a screening for family violence in families with whom they mediate.

This process allows for the exclusion of some families from mediation with a referral back to court as well as the implementation of special safeguards in some cases, such as the use of co-mediators, separate sessions with the spouses, or mediation by telephone (Thoennes et al., 1995).

TREATMENT OF THE PERPETRATOR

Perpetrators of family violence may seek mental health services to help them change their pattern of aggression. In many of these cases, perpetrators are court-mandated to receive therapy (Famularo, Kinscherff, Bunshaft, Spivak, & Fenton, 1989). Clearly, these individuals are in need of treatment, and the courts are to be commended for their action. However, in our clinical practice, we have frequently observed two problems for clinicians in this situation.

First, the perpetrators sometimes have little motivation to actively address their individual adjustment issues and may prefer to use therapy to "vent" about their problems, including costs incurred by legal expenses, the fact that their problems are caused by others, or the unjust nature of the court system, which they sometimes view as biased against males.

Second, these individuals are unlikely to attend therapy for long (Famularo et al., 1989), thus calling into question the benefits they receive from treatment.

Third, although the court may mandate that therapy occur, specific goals or targets for intervention often are not identified. Thus clinicians treating court-mandated or court-referred persons who have committed family violence may not have clear treatment goals established by either the client or the courts. As such, the initial step is to aid the client in the process of selecting appropriate and feasible therapy goals. For example, anger management may be the focus of treatment for many persons who are violent. Treatment for chemical dependency may also be recommended for people whose substance use is out of control or seems to influence their aggression (Jurich, 1990), and it may be court-mandated (Famularo et al., 1989).

The Importance of Displaying Sensitivity

Regardless of the point in the family where intervention occurs, it is usually crucial that clinicians not demean the perpetrator or the family unit (Gentry & Eaddy, 1980), which could contribute to already high treatment dropout rates (Grusznski & Carrillo, 1988). Many clinicians have pointed out that blaming the perpetrator for the violence often serves only to increase his or her defensiveness and subsequent aggressiveness (Gerbi, 1994). Thus, when working with the perpetrator, a stance that is firm, but not punitive, may yield the most clinical benefit (Gentry & Eaddy, 1980). Initially, a high degree of expressed empathy, as long as it does not serve to reinforce the client's abusive tendencies, can allow a clinician to "hook" the perpetrator into therapy and place the therapist, after a solid therapeutic relationship has been formed, in a position to challenge the client and his use of aggression (Jurich, 1990).

Often, perpetrators of violence within a family were themselves victims of violence when they were children (Gerbi, 1994). Breaking this cycle of intergenerational violence thus becomes a primary goal of therapeutic intervention. In a study of parents who had been abused during their childhoods, nonabusive parents seemed to "recognize the effects parental abuse had on them as well as its potential effects on current child-rearing patterns" (Egeland, Jacobvitz, & Sroufe, 1988, p. 1087). Thus it makes sense intuitively that training in perspective-taking and empathy may be beneficial when working with perpetrators who have a history of abuse. Additionally, therapists may be able to be more empathic and effective in working with violent individuals if the therapists are able to view them not as monsters but as persons who lack certain skills and can be helped via intervention.

Another technique that can be helpful is using the perpetrator's statements that clash with his or her violent behavior, such as a desire to be a suitable role model for the children (Gerbi, 1994). Redefining aggression as a weakness rather than a strength, a loss of control instead of a show of force, may also expedite change in the perpetrator (Gerbi, 1994).

Education/Behavioral Management

Often, parents who abuse their children have inadequate or inaccurate knowledge concerning normal child development (Jurich, 1990; Yegidis, 1992). Additionally, parents who are abusive frequently have a limited child discipline repertoire. Thus education with abusive parents often concerns information pertaining to difficult child developmental periods as well as more positive methods of child behavioral management.

Seven early difficult periods are commonly identified: colic, awakening at night, separation anxiety, normal exploratory behavior, normal negativism, normal poor appetite, and toilet training resistance (Schmitt, 1987). These difficult child periods can cause stress and frustration in parents. Providing parents with alternative behaviors to abuse serves to decrease abuse and increase the parental sense of control over their actions. By normalizing these periods, parents can begin to view their children's behavior as normal versus oppositional. For parents of adolescents, who may view their youngster as oppositional, the clinician can reframe the adolescent's behavior as attempts to acquire a sense of independence and construct a more mature personal identity.

Behavioral management training involves assisting parents in developing systems of rules, rewards, and punishment (Schmitt, 1987) and can help parents learn to interact with their children in a more positive manner (Wolfe, Sandler, & Kaufman, 1981). Spanking and other forms of physical aggression should be strictly discouraged. However, some parents refuse to relinquish spanking from their behavioral management system. In these cases, clinicians should provide parents with eight rules concerning restriction on physical punishment: (a) spank with an open hand, (b) only hit the buttocks or hand, (c) do not swat more than once, (d) do not spank children before they are old enough to walk, (e) do not spank more than once a day, (f) do not spank for child aggression, (g) do not ever shake children, and (h) use time-out or other techniques before using spankings (Schmitt, 1987). This system, although inferior to total abstention from physical punishment, may help prevent child injury.

Anger Management

Persons who are violent within the family often lack the skills to control their anger or cope with it in a socially acceptable manner. For these clients, training in anger management can be beneficial in the process of becoming nonviolent (Saunders, 1996). The initial goal here is aiding the abuser in identifying triggers for his or her anger (e.g., child misbehavior, stress) and cues (e.g., physiological symptoms) that may alert him or her to the buildup of anger and aggressive feelings (Grusznski & Carrillo, 1988). Next, with the help of the clinician, the client can learn strategies for coping with this anger (Grusznski & Carrillo, 1988). These tactics can vary widely for different people, including counting to ten, relaxation techniques, thought stopping and positive self-talk, and talking to close friends. A little creativity is probably necessary at this point.

Biological Interventions

Biological approaches to treatment involve the use of psychopharmacology and endeavor to regulate aggressive behaviors by modifying brain chemicals or hormonal disruptions (Burrowes et al., 1988). For aggression that results from a person's psychotic ideation, antipsychotics are generally used (Yudofsky et al., 1995). Clonazapam or other antianxiety agents may be used when aggression occurs in conjunction with severe anxiety (Yudofsky et al., 1995). Antimanic medications, such as lithium, may also be useful for the control of violence (Yudofsky et al., 1995). By identifying and treating underlying psychiatric disorders, clinicians may be able to diminish aggressive behavior in certain individuals, and additional interventions can help generalize treatment gains.

The use of beta-blockers, such as propranolol, in persons with intermittent explosive disorder has shown some initial promise (Brizer, 1988) and merits further attention. The use of pharmacology for family violence is generally recommended only as part of a multifaceted treatment program that may also include behavioral interventions, family therapy, occupational therapy, or couples counseling (Yudofsky et al., 1995). Additional research examining the possible biological causes of violence may help bring about new treatments.

TREATMENT OF THE CHILD WHO HAS BEEN ABUSED WITHIN THE FAMILY

Treatment for the child can take place in a variety of settings, including a traditional clinic, crisis nursery, play school program, and out-of-home placement, such as foster care (Gelles & Maynard, 1987). Intervention with children who have been abused generally requires a multicomponent treatment that addresses the numerous problems they may exhibit.

The primary goal is to address the child's symptoms and bolster his or her ability to cope with the situation. When treatment is provided directly to the child, the clinician's secondary goal is to end the cycle of intergenerational violence (Hughes, 1982). Throughout treatment, empathy must be displayed for the child and his or her feelings. Ensuring the child's psychological security in session by providing an emotionally safe environment will greatly facilitate effective treatment (van Dalen & Glasserman, 1997). Violent families often object to displays or discussions of feelings or emotions. Thus an initial goal for therapy may be educating the child about various feelings and helping him or her label the experience of abuse (Giller, 1990).

Safety Issues

The most pressing issue for therapy with the abused child is ensuring that the child is safe from present and future abuse. Regardless of the circumstances, the child victim of family violence needs to be provided with immediate protection from the deleterious physical and psychological impact of familial aggression (Gentry & Eaddy, 1980). Additionally, this safety must be secured before formal treatment can be initiated to help the child address problems arising from the abuse (Gentry & Eaddy, 1980). This beginning process is likely to be the responsibility primarily of legal authorities or child protection agencies and may involve removing the child or the perpetrator from the home. However, other mental health professionals may be involved in various ways. For example, a clinician, such as a child psychologist or psychiatrist, may be the first person outside of the family to become aware of abuse or potential abuse. If abuse is documented or even suspected, mental health professionals are required by law to make a report via the national child abuse hot line (Brosig & Kalichman, 1992).

In some cases, particularly where severe abuse has occurred, the abuser may be in prison or may be permanently removed from the household through other means. This situation communicates to the abuser that he or she cannot continue to be violent, and that if he or she is violent, then there will be negative consequences meted out by society (Yegidis, 1992). However, in situations where the abuse was mild or moderate, carefully supervised contact with the perpetrator may actually be beneficial and may assist the child in resolving issues related to abuse as well as helping the family address their problems in a more realistic manner (Gentry & Eaddy, 1980). Even if the perpetrator is removed from the home, this situation probably will not be permanent, and the child's long-term safety must be considered (Gentry & Eaddy, 1980). Long-term safety issues revolve around teaching the child to avoid future abuse.

Increasing Social Support

One important factor in determining the long-term effects of child abuse appears to be the involvement in the child's life of a caring and nurturing adult (Kashani, Rosenberg, Beck, Reid, & Battle, 1987). This point was documented by Egeland and colleagues (1988), who found that, when compared with abusive mothers who had been abused in childhood, nonabusive mothers who had been abused in childhood more often reported having experienced a supportive relationship with an adult during childhood.

One therapy goal therefore may involve strengthening the relationship between the child and his or her nonabusive parent. The parent may be taught parenting skills, positive ways of showing affection, and nonviolent behavioral management techniques (e.g., time-out, rewards). In some cases, the nonabusive parent may not be able to fulfill this role. Thus a therapeutic goal in working with children who have been abused is helping the children gain access to such an individual. For example, the child may be encouraged to spend time with an appropriate adult relative (e.g., grandparent, aunt, or uncle) or to join an organization such as Big Brothers/Big Sisters or some other type of mentorship program.

Post-Traumatic Stress Disorder

Some children who are abused may go on to develop post-traumatic stress disorder (PTSD). Cognitive-behavioral therapy (CBT) is one promising form of intervention commonly employed for this problem (Yule & Canterbury, 1994). As with CBT employed with other anxiety disorders, CBT for PTSD focuses primarily on exposure of the child to feared situations (Bell-Dolan & Allan, in press; Lipovsky, 1991). Abreaction, or the retelling of the trauma in the child's own words, can be used for this purpose. A fear hierarchy should also be constructed consisting of at least 10 items related to the family violence (e.g., being around adult males). Imaginal exposure, paired with relaxation techniques, can then be used.

Cognitive techniques can be used to help the youngster identify, evaluate, and challenge maladaptive thoughts the child may have because of abuse (Lipovsky, 1991). In particular, the child may blame him- or herself for the family violence. Feelings of guilt and shame are also common (Sonnenberg, 1988) in PTSD and can be treated via cognitive therapy. The clinician can, via cognitive procedures, help the child change these beliefs and replace them with more adaptive thoughts.

However, because of the traumatic nature of the events associated with the abuse, it is preferable to "build up" the child as much as possible before exposure is initiated. For example, the child's social network may be bolstered to provide him or her with outlets for discussing upsetting situations that occur outside of therapy (Bell-Dolan & Allan, in press). Additionally, the child may be taught about different emotions and ways of expressing feelings. After this initial stage, exposure can commence. For abuse-related trauma, imaginal exposure most likely will be necessary and should involve having the child tell about specific incidents of abuse in detail.

Psychopharmacology is helpful in some cases of adult PTSD (Sonnenberg, 1988) but has not been examined extensively for children or adolescents with PTSD.

Depression

One of the conditions most commonly displayed by children who have been abused is depression in the form of depressive symptoms, dysthymic disorder, or the full syndrome of major depression. Fortunately, a number of treatment interventions have been developed to help remediate child and adolescent depression.

Cognitive-behavioral therapy is often a useful intervention for children or adolescents who are depressed. One manual that has documented efficacy is the *Adolescent Coping With Depression Course* by Clarke, Lewinsohn, and Hops (1990). This protocol was originally developed for use with adolescent groups but is frequently adapted for use with individual children or adolescents. Based on the social reinforcement theory of depression, the program incorporates a number of cognitive-behavioral techniques such as social skills training, pleasant activities scheduling, relaxation, cognitive restructuring, communication skills training, and problem-solving training. Cognitive restructuring may be particularly helpful in addressing children's maladaptive thoughts concerning their role in the violence, such as thinking that they caused the abuse to occur (Jaffe, Hurley, & Wolfe, 1990).

Another form of individual therapy sometimes used with youngsters is interpersonal psychotherapy (e.g., Mufson, Moreau, Weissman, & Klerman, 1993). This intervention is based on the assumption that "depression is inextricably intertwined with the patient's interpersonal relationships" (Mufson et al., 1993, p. 3). Hence the primary goal of therapy is the improvement of the youth's current interpersonal relationships. When treating the child, the clinician can serve as a positive model of adult-child relations. During adolescence, many role transitions occur that can become problematic for an adolescent's parent-child relations. Thus a therapist may focus on helping the adolescent mourn the loss of the old role and accepting positive aspects of the new role. For the child who has been abused and removed from the home, many new roles will replace older ones. Additionally, the child may exhibit grief and loss in relation to the dissolution of the family (Yegidis, 1992), which can be tackled via interpersonal therapy.

Psychopharmacology, including SSRIs and tricyclics, has shown some results with childhood depression. However, we generally prefer to use other forms of intervention first. Typically, medications are used after other forms of intervention have been unsuccessful or if the depression is extreme and the child is in danger of self-harm behaviors.

TREATMENT OF THE CHILD WHO HAS WITNESSED FAMILY VIOLENCE

Although for many years mental health professionals have been well aware of the negative impact of child abuse, the effects of witnessing family violence have only recently been appreciated (Wilson, Cameron, Jaffe, & Wolfe, 1989). Not surprisingly, then, treatment for the problem has lagged behind.

Many different protocols have been designed to address the unique problems faced by children who have witnessed violence within the home. Many of these treatments have little empirical documentation, but, notably, clinicians working at the forefront of this problem have indicated that they may be beneficial. However, ongoing research documenting the effectiveness of these programs is needed and may stimulate new and more efficacious protocols.

Safety Issues

As with the child who has been abused, safety issues need to be addressed immediately for the child who has witnessed family violence (Hurley & Jaffe, 1990; Jaffe et al., 1990). The perpetrator may return to the home or the abused spouse may enter another relationship with a violent individual, putting the spouse and child in future danger. In some cases, the abused spouse will return voluntarily to the abuser. Persons who are abused will frequently leave the relationship many times before the departure becomes permanent. In assessing this likelihood, the clinician can assess a number of important questions (Wetzel & Ross, 1983): Has the person left before? What is the extent of his or her plans to leave? What are the person's current feelings toward the abuser? Does the person realize the risks of reuniting? The child in these types of families needs to be taught protection skills to ward off potential abuse. Problem solving can be used with the child to help him or her generate plans for escaping from future dangerous situations. For example, the child may elect to go to the house of a trusted neighbor or call the police.

Group Format

Many clinicians suggest the use of a group format for the treatment of child witnesses to family violence (e.g., Peled & Davis, 1995; Wilson et al., 1989). In particular, it may be helpful to have female and male cotherapists serve as models of appropriate male-female relations (Wilson et al., 1989), something these children may lack in their everyday lives.

Wilson and colleagues (1989) have outlined a detailed treatment protocol that focuses on education and prevention (see also Peled & Davis, 1995). Specific goals include helping the children to (a) develop new and more adaptive responses to past experiences, (b) learn problem solving, (c) examine their responsibility for behavior, (d) evaluate the effectiveness of aggression as a means of conflict resolution, and (e) boost their self-esteem. The 10-session program incorporates a variety of cognitive-behavioral and experiential techniques. A brief summary of the 10 sessions follows:

1. The first session is used to encourage the child to talk about the family violence, which can be difficult because the violence is likely to have been a "family secret" not shared with outsiders. Learning that other children have experienced family violence in their homes can have a powerful impact on children. The different types of family violence (e.g., spousal versus child abuse) are also discussed.

2. The second session focuses on affect and helping children label their feelings. The children generate a list of many feelings, which are then defined and situations are discussed for which the feelings may occur.

3. During the third session, the group discusses healthy and unhealthy ways of expressing anger. Role-plays are used to help the kids gain experience in solving problems without using anger. Relaxation procedures are also taught.

4. Responsibility issues are addressed in session four. Children are taught to identify their degree of responsibility in different areas in their lives, including areas of low responsibility, such as fighting between their parents, and areas of high responsibility, such as relationships with peers. Safety issues are also explored and the children develop plans for avoiding violence in their homes in the future.

5. Session five concerns the positive facets of the children's current social support systems and ways in which they can expand their network.

6. Self-esteem is targeted in session six, when children identify positive and negative aspects of themselves. The children also discuss ways that they are like and unlike their parents so as to integrate all of these pieces. One intriguing method that can be used is the "life-puzzle" task. The child is provided with construction paper that is cut into four interlocking pieces representing how the child feels at home, with peers, at school, and in therapy group. The child then colors the four pieces and discusses how he or she feels in each situation and how he or she views him- or herself in that setting. The pieces are then put together and emphasis is placed on having the child trying to integrate the different pieces of him- or herself.

7. Responsibility is addressed again, specifically in relation to the aggression displayed by the children's parents. Parental actions are labeled "adult issues" and the child is told that children cannot take responsibility for these actions. Children in the group then tell stories about incidents that happened in their families, and actions are appropriately identified as being the responsibility of certain individuals (e.g., a parent).

8. The children are educated about the widespread nature of family violence, and the concept of the cyclical nature of violence is discussed. Sometimes children are afraid of their anger and think that they will become violent like their parent(s) (Jaffe et al., 1990). The children are encouraged to discuss their parents' methods of handling anger and then their own means of expressing anger.

9. Session nine focuses on wishes the children have about their families. Specifically, the children enumerate activities that they like and do not like to do with their parents. Issues surrounding parental separation or divorce are also processed, including visitation, feelings of conflict when placed between the parents, and accepting their parents' new relationships. This discussion can be advanced via having the children draw pictures of their family in the past, present, and future.

10. Control is highlighted in the final session and the children are encouraged to identify ways in which they have control over their own lives. Finally, the children discuss positive characteristics of their relationships with various people in their social support network, including parents, siblings, and friends.

The authors of this protocol (Wilson et al., 1989) note that family violence is often a "family secret" and that many kids presenting for treatment have never discussed the problem with anyone outside of their immediate families. Accordingly, some children may be hesitant to talk about these issues in a group or even with an individual therapist. One technique the protocol authors have found helpful in counteracting this dilemma is to have the parent(s) give the child verbal permission to talk about the family, which can help alleviate the child's sense of disloyalty. Although this protocol was developed for use with a group, it can be easily adapted and used with individual children or adolescents who have witnessed familial abuse. Additionally, particular components can be discarded or expanded based on the needs of the child or adolescent.

FAMILY THERAPY FOR
THE VIOLENT FAMILY

Family therapy with families who have been violent may include the entire family, the nonabusive parent and the children, or any other number of forms. It is based on the assumption that violence is a systemic problem (Gentry & Eaddy, 1980). Specifically, the characteristics of living in a family, such as emotional closeness and high physical proximity to others, may result in a great deal of frustration and stress for some people, which may be discharged through violence (Gentry & Eaddy, 1980). Additionally, violence is often affiliated with or results in other significant problems within the family (Wolfe & Bourdeau, 1987). Based on this view, effective treatment must intervene at all levels of the family system, including the children, the nonabusing parent, and the perpetrator(s) (Gentry & Eaddy, 1980). In general, a family systems approach may be most useful for addressing family violence because, if intervention is made in only one part of the system (e.g., treating the perpetrator), the family's homeostatic processes may intensify and cause other family members to sabotage treatment to maintain the family's status quo, even though it may ultimately be damaging to the family (Gentry & Eaddy, 1980).

Generally, the perpetrator of violence within the family has been removed and family therapy will be used for purposes of reunification. In other cases, the clinician will become aware after family therapy has been initiated of a pattern of intrafamilial violence that may require reporting. Here, the primary goal for the clinician is to stop the violence (Willbach, 1989).

In terms of a general systemic approach, when working with an entire family, each member should be allowed and encouraged to discuss his or her experiences in the family. This technique will help make everyone feel like part of the process but may also provide an opportunity for the therapist to actively observe family interaction patterns and dynamics (Jurich, 1990).

A structural family systems approach has been applied in treating the violent family. The therapist's role involves confronting the family's interactional style and surreptitious rules that dominate the family's interactions (Gelles & Maynard, 1987). The family is then encouraged to jettison unyielding patterns of interactions that have become maladaptive (Gelles & Maynard, 1987). Specifically, the clinician aids the parents in establishing proper boundaries between family members and appropriate hierarchies between the parents and children as well as improving marital communication (Gelles & Maynard, 1987).

In general, the violent family will require a great deal of crisis intervention and will not likely be the type of client who can be seen only once a week (Yegidis, 1992). Additional or telephone sessions sometimes may be necessary.

The Nonviolence Contract

A helpful tool sometimes used by family therapists when working with aggressive individuals or families is the nonviolence contract (Bell & Chance-

Hill, 1991; Willbach, 1989). Basically, the perpetrator is requested to make and/or sign a contract agreeing that the family violence will cease immediately. In return, the clinician assents to provide family therapy. If the abuser cannot agree to the contract, then individual therapy for the perpetrator is provided instead and family therapy is not offered (Willbach, 1989). In contrast to the nonviolence contract, one family systems approach to family violence involves not directly setting the goal with the family of ceasing the violence immediately. Instead, the clinician uses indirect methods, such as paradox (Willbach, 1989). However, there seems to be an inherent danger in this approach and we generally recommend a more direct stance. Of course, if child abuse is present, a report must be made regardless of the clinician's orientation.

Reunification

Reunification is often the goal of family therapy with violent families. Some clinicians may have a propensity to advocate against reunification in such cases. However, eventual familial reunification, particularly in less severe cases of family violence, may actually be better for children than permanently separating the perpetrator from the family. If the perpetrator is removed permanently from the home, the child may experience loss and confusion. In contrast, if reunification is possible and the perpetrator actively pursues therapy and attempts positive change, then the child is provided with a model of effective coping (Giller, 1990) and is given the message that the family is worth trying to save (Gentry & Eaddy, 1980). Given the emphasis on reunification by the legal and child protective services systems, clinicians need to be aware of family therapy techniques, such as problem-solving and communication training, that may be useful for helping families reunify in a healthy and safe manner.

Increasing Positive Interactions
and Social Support

Families who are violent tend to be marked by a notable lack of positive interactions in the form of conversations, cooperation, and sharing (Gerbi, 1994). Consequently, an initial goal for family therapy frequently consists of increasing shared, pleasant activities. For example, having a family undertake activities that are pleasurable to all members, such as going to the park or having dinner together, can help increase positive affect. In turn, the increase in enjoyment can promote greater motivation for the family to attain further therapeutic advances. Lovell and Richey (1991) describe a social-support-skill training protocol that they have used with parents who are at risk for violence. This intervention focuses on increasing parental social support. For example, parents are encouraged to develop adult friendships to help ease tension and stress as well as remediate the isolated nature of the core family.

Problem-Solving and Communication Training

Some members of families who have poor conflict resolution skills may tend to use violence as a "default" method for solving problems within the family (Gentry & Eaddy, 1980). When a conflict arises in violent families, members tend to have limited responses in their repertoire (Gerbi, 1994). Additionally, decision making tends to be done by one or a few persons, and other family members are not involved (Straus et al., 1980). Accordingly, a crucial aspect of treatment with many families who have experienced violence is training in problem solving or conflict resolution involving the entire family. The goals of this training are (a) to help remediate current problems and (b) to aid the parents and children in becoming more flexible in solving problems. Additionally, during problem-solving training, the clinician serves as a model for the family of an adult with skills in resolving conflict in a nonviolent manner (Giller, 1990). This type of therapy may also be used to help the family establish a visitation plan (Yegidis, 1992).

Foster and Robin (1989) have outlined an intervention called "Problem-Solving Communication Training" that entails five steps.

First, the family defines the problem that is troublesome. The family should be encouraged to state the problem in a form that addresses actions, feelings, or situations and does not put blame on another family member. Each family member is persuaded to define the problem as well as paraphrase the definitions given by the other individuals in the family.

Second, after the problem has been adequately defined, the family brainstorms and generates multiple solutions to the problem. The family is encouraged to be creative in generating solutions. Thus any solution is acceptable at this point and the family should refrain from evaluating the solutions during this stage. These solutions should be recorded by either the therapist or a family member. Generally, the therapist should abstain from providing solutions unless the family is unable to commence this stage by their own volition.

Third, the solutions are evaluated by the family through the enumeration of positive and negative potential consequences for each solution with each family member giving the resolution a plus or a minus. The therapist facilitates this process by encouraging individuals to consider the perspectives of other family members. If consensus is reached about a solution, then it is retained or deleted. If consensus is not reached, then the therapist should encourage further discussion of the solution as well as compromise and negotiation. The remaining solutions are then examined, and compromise and negotiation are used to help select a final solution.

Fourth, the chosen solution is discussed, and implementation is planned. The plan should be carefully defined in terms of specific behaviors. The therapist may also mention some possible obstacles to executing the plan to help the family plan ahead and have a greater chance of success. The family is then sent off to undertake the solution.

Fifth, after the family has attempted to perform the plan, the therapist reviews the results with the family. If the solution worked and a problem no longer exists, then the therapist should generously praise the family and help them celebrate their success. If the solution did not work and a problem still exists, then the therapist should generously praise the family's effort, and problem solving should be re-initiated to help find a new plan. After the family acquires the ability to solve problems without the use of aggression or conflict, the likelihood of family violence presumably will decrease.

This process can be used to aid the family in developing a new set of rules for the children (Jurich, 1990), which may be necessary if the family had been operating with an overly restrictive framework. By soliciting participation from the children, their self-esteem and sense of control can be bolstered as well as the likelihood that they will agree with and follow the rules (Jurich, 1990).

SUMMARY

A number of beneficial treatment modalities have been developed to intervene with the violent family. Education and problem solving seem to be keys across these methods as violence appears to stem largely from deficiencies in knowledge about normal child development as well as the ability to solve problems without conflict. Additionally, family therapy is generally recommended due to the fact that family violence appears to be largely a systemic problem. Although many of these techniques have some documented efficacy, the field as a whole seems to suffer from a lack of outcome studies using appropriate control groups, large sample sizes, and multiple informants to measure progress.

9

THE RESILIENT CHILD AND PREVENTION STRATEGIES

LESSONS FROM
THE RESILIENT CHILD

Many children who are raised in violent families largely seem to avoid the negative sequelae normally associated with such an environment. These "stress-resilient" children dodge the pitfalls of their chaotic homes and develop into competent adults (Kashani, Rosenberg, et al., 1987). Studying these children may provide insight into putative protective factors for children in violent homes.

A study (Kashani, Rosenberg, et al., 1987) we conducted in the general population examined "well-adjusted" adolescents who did not meet criteria for a DSM diagnosis and did not require treatment for any dysfunctional behaviors or thoughts; only 16.7% of our sample fit this definition. These adolescents differed from their maladjusted peers in a number of ways. First, they came from higher SES families. Second, they reported fewer life stressors (e.g., family moves). Third, they indicated that they had a more developed social support system and described their parents as more "caring." In another study (Kashani & Shepherd, 1990), we found that adolescents with a larger number of people in their social support system were less likely than their less supported peers to report using maladaptive conflict resolution measures (e.g., verbal or violent aggression).

The social support system of the youngster from a violent family appears to be crucial in determining the impact that the violence will wield on the child (Valentine & Feinauer, 1993; Watt, David, Ladd, & Shamos, 1995). Resilient children seem to have people to whom they can turn for emotional support when it is needed. Additionally, resilient children and adolescents tend to develop a secure attachment with either the nonviolent parent or some other significant adult (Katsikas et al., 1996; Neighbors, Forehand, & McVicar, 1993).

Self-esteem also emerges as a potentially critical differentiator between resilient and nonresilient adolescents who have witnessed considerable conflict between their parents or experienced maltreatment (Cicchetti, Rogosch, Lynch, & Holt, 1993; Neighbors et al., 1993). Children with high self-esteem in one area (e.g., school performance) may focus on and build upon that domain, which allows them more easily to "escape" their family violence. However, causality cannot be conclusively inferred in this relationship and resilience in the face of hardship could actually lead to increased self-esteem, although this pathway seems less likely than high self-esteem leading to resilience.

Although the majority of research in the family violence literature examines the detrimental impact of family violence on children and adolescents, insight into the nature of violent families can also be provided via investigations of those youngsters who successfully surmount this adversity (Neighbors et al., 1993). To date, social support and self-esteem have materialized as such factors and merit further examination as targets of intervention and prevention.

PREVENTION STRATEGIES

A final area related to family violence to be discussed involves prevention. Research on family violence has focused on a number of risk factors. Monahan (1996) aptly asserts that "managing risk as well as assessing risk must be a goal of research" (p. 115). We strongly agree with this statement, and this section will discuss some relevant preventive measures aimed at realizing that goal. Research on prevention has generally lagged behind intervention efforts, and most early prevention programs were not systematically evaluated for efficacy (Barth, Ash, & Hacking, 1986); however, several noteworthy topics merit discussion.

In our review, we will start first with the lessons learned from the resilient child. Considering the social support component that seems to lead to resilience, children from at-risk families can be encouraged to develop supportive relationships with family members or extrafamilial persons. This process could take a number of forms. Children's self-esteem can also become a target of preventive measures. These measures could range from primary prevention where attempts are made on a community, state, or national basis to bolster children's self-esteem, to secondary prevention where the self-esteem of at-risk populations (e.g., the poor, single-parent households) is targeted, to tertiary prevention involving family therapy and self-enhancing techniques for persons who have become violent.

Primary Prevention

Many adults who perpetrate family violence are ignorant of normal child development and have poor coping and problem-solving skills. Thus education seems to be a key component of successful primary prevention. For example, in schools, children and adolescents can be taught about child development so that when they become parents, they will have an accurate depiction of what to expect from their own children (Feindler & Becker, 1994; Starr, 1979). Teaching children how to solve problems effectively without using violence or aggression can also be useful in preventing later family violence.

As discussed in Chapter 3, cases of fatal child abuse are commonly precipitated by developmentally normal child behaviors, such as having an accident during toilet training. We therefore would like to propose that pregnant women and the fathers of their children, in particular, should be required to attend educational classes that can teach them what to expect when having a baby. When the parents are young, these preventive techniques may be especially important and can include training about how to select baby-sitters given that young parents often leave their children with other young persons who have little knowledge about child care or development (Klerman, 1993). Normal development from infancy, toddlerhood, preschool, and elementary school through adolescence can be discussed so that parents can understand what is ordinary for children.

Drawing from the observations others (e.g., Levinson, 1989) have made regarding societies without violence (see Chapter 6), we would like to posit a few tentative ideas for prevention. Most important, from an early age, children should be taught problem-solving and negotiation/compromise skills. One of the keys to avoiding violence appears to be the presence of the ability to solve conflict in a verbal, as opposed to physical, manner. Additionally, equality between males and females needs continued emphasis in our society.

Secondary Prevention

A person who is violent to his or her spouse or children often was raised in a family that was unable to meet his or her basic needs and parent him or her effectively (Gilbert, 1996). Parents who are violent in the family frequently have been raised in homes that were characterized by excessive violence. Thus a secondary prevention technique involves intervening with children from violent households to help prevent the intergenerational transmission of violence. Mental health professionals can help prevent the propagation of family violence by actively providing clinical services to this underserved population.

For example, clinicians could supply treatment to children in battered women's shelters or consultation to such shelters regarding potentially helpful techniques or programs. Families in rural areas also experience family violence at high rates and can benefit from programs developed by mental health professionals (Edelson & Frank, 1991). Community needs assessment, consisting of surveying various persons (e.g., community leaders, school officials, clergy, and average citizens) in a rural community, can help provide information about specific problematic attitudes or resource deficits (e.g., lack of women's shelters) for intervention (Edelson & Frank, 1991).

Another preventive measure, particularly in cases of divorce, involves improving the relationship between the couple to help assuage negative feelings between them, particularly the desire to gain revenge. Marital or couples counseling can help them settle salient differences and keep the children from being put in the middle of conflicts (Nesbit & Karagianis, 1987).

Prevention of Intrafamilial Homicide

As we noted in Chapter 4, violence within the home sometimes leads to homicide. Based on our forensic research (Kashani, Darby, et al., 1997) with homicidal adolescents, we have identified a few preventive techniques for mental health professionals that may be helpful in preventing deadly violence in such families, particularly when sibling violence is at a high level.

1. Denounce the sensationalism of force and violence. Murder and violent acts are sometimes sensationalized in the media, which results in a murderer receiving substantial attention. In contrast, the victims of family violence are soon forgotten. We are reminded of a clinical case we saw a few years ago. Lisa was a 16-year-old adolescent female who seemed to thrive on being violent. One night she and her boyfriend beat a homeless man "for fun." Lisa's self-professed primary goal in life was to become the first female serial killer because she knew that she would become famous and gain recognition.

2. Discourage the presence of guns in homes. In homes with family violence, guns should be removed. Weapons can be used impulsively by children or adults with devastating effects.

3. Deemphasize symbols of status. We have found that the acquisition of status symbols as well as the use of the family car can be a tremendous source of familial conflict.

4. Use the extended family to help prevent violence. Chaotic families tend to be under a great deal of stress. Often, the family is described as "isolated" and not having much contact with extended family members. If available, support from extended family members can help ease the strain in a family.

5. Make parents aware of the putative destructive impact of sibling rivalry. We have studied several juveniles who murdered a sibling. In a disorganized family, sibling rivalry can advance to the point of extreme hatred and violence. Parents should be encouraged to dissuade siblings from being competitive, emphasize the importance of cooperation between family members, and avoid making unfavorable comparisons between siblings

SUMMARY

Although a few preventive strategies have been outlined, to date, little research has been conducted that has explicitly examined potential protective factors that serve to prevent family violence, and more research is needed in this important area to help guide development of preventive measures (see Chapter 10 for a discussion of future research ideas). Too often research has focused on identifying risk, as opposed to protective, factors.

However, the resilient child can teach us a number of lessons about family violence. First, social support within the family or from external sources can influence the impact that family violence has on children and adolescents. Researchers and mental health professionals need to take the next step and determine how the problem of family violence can be prevented. We have drawn some ideas for prevention from the literature, including efforts to halt the intergenerational transmission of violence. Other methods have been proposed based on our experience and the extant empirical data. Regarding risk and protective factors, education seems to be a particularly important tool and ideally should be implemented in school curricula.

10

DISCUSSION AND FUTURE DIRECTIONS FOR RESEARCH

DISCUSSION

Today's children face threats from a multitude of sources, including disease, gang violence, sexual abuse, and street violence. Perhaps none is more insidious than the threat of family violence, which has become a way of life for many children (Ryan, 1995). Conceptualized as a stressor, family violence is clearly a severe one as it affects the child on a daily basis and tends to be chronic (Wolfe & Jaffe, 1991). In 1994, Dr. Robert McAfee, president of the American Medical Association, proposed that family violence is a disease (Goldman, 1994). Similarly, Dr. Lawrence Stone, president of the American Academy of Child and Adolescent Psychiatry, compared violence to a contagious disease (Turkel, 1996). We agree with these statements.

Intrafamilial aggression appears to be a relatively common occurrence that cuts across socioeconomic, educational, and racial categories. No type of family seems immune from violence within that system. Indeed, when writing this book, we were dismayed by the prevalence of family violence in the cases we have seen. Even focusing primarily on children we have treated during the past 2-3 years, we were easily able to recall cases that illustrate nearly every major point in this book.

The effects of family violence were initially examined in relation to battered spouses, especially women. However, gradually the focus has turned to children and adolescents. Today, family violence is recognized as a consequential problem for society, one that seems to affect a number of short- and long-term outcomes on children and adolescents. The two main types that are typically examined include abuse perpetrated by parents upon children and adolescents and the vicarious observation of familial violence (e.g., wife battering) by youths. Additionally, abuse by siblings and observing violence directed toward the elderly represent other forms of family violence. This book has focused on examining research that explores the complex pattern of effects family violence can have on children. What our review confirms is that the impact of family violence can be observed in numerous spheres of child functioning or development (Emery, 1989). The most common factors that have been studied include cognitive, behavioral, social, and emotional functioning (Kashani et al., 1992). Consistently, empirical data confirm that experiencing or witnessing family violence exerts a negative impact on children's functioning in these areas.

However, it appears that a youngster's response to family violence may be influenced by several important intrafamilial and extrafamilial considerations, including support and nurturing from other family members and social support outside the family. Additionally, child characteristics, such as age, developmental level, premorbid intelligence, gender, and resilience, may affect this relationship.

A number of treatment modalities have been outlined in the literature and summarized here. These interventions target the anxiety and depressive symptoms children may experience in relation to familial abuse. Prevention, however, would seem to be a more beneficial approach. Now that researchers have identified factors that put families at risk for violence, intervening before violence becomes notable and destructive, although admittedly a difficult task, is the next step. The home environment should be safe for children, and child mental health professionals should make this goal a primary one in their research and clinical work.

PROBLEMS AND FUTURE DIRECTIONS FOR RESEARCH

Although the literature on family violence is growing rapidly and a great deal is known about this phenomenon, a number of crucial issues have not yet been addressed. This section is intended to spur and guide future research in this area. Three major areas will be considered: methodological considerations, sampling considerations, and overlooked topics.

Methodological Considerations

Much of the research conducted in this area and reviewed in this book is correlational in nature, preventing us from discerning cause-and-effect relationships. Longitudinal studies can help remediate this problem and allow stronger conclusions to be derived. Large studies conducted on the general population will also help identify the nature and degree of family violence in our society as well as the impact it has on children and adolescents who witness or experience varying degrees of family violence. Davis (1988) suggests that the duration, versus the degree, of family violence should also be considered as a separate issue and investigated systematically.

An issue discussed in Chapter 7 concerns the questionable validity of data collected from the children in a violent family who may perceive a need to protect the privacy of the family. One potential solution to this problem that has been underused is assessing the impact of violence on children and adolescents through projective techniques (Kilpatrick & Lockhart, 1991). We acknowledge that projective testing is the source of heated debate among clinicians and researchers and may have less than optimal validity. However, we have found projective methods (e.g., Three Wishes, Rorschach) useful in our clinical work and think that using them in family violence research could help further delineate some important issues. Alternatively, interviewing multiple family members separately and via standardized interview protocols may help increase the validity of self-reports (Kilpatrick & Lockhart, 1991).

A final methodological issue that merits attention concerns the use of group designs. Specifically, most empirical research on familial abuse uses multivariate or other group comparison approaches. These studies allow for the examination of various group differences (e.g., physical versus sexual abuse, male versus female). However, idiographic effects of family violence on particular types of children are rarely explored. The specific factors that protect some children from developing psychopathology and put others at risk are still fairly unknown. Thus carefully controlled case studies and investigations of subgroups of children who have witnessed or experienced family violence could be useful.

Sampling Considerations

Mothers' reports of their children's psychopathology have dominated the literature. Of course, such reports are of great interest; however, in some families the mother may also be a perpetrator of violence. Conversely, in cases of spousal violence, the mothers' distress due to being abused, particularly if they are residing in shelters, may bias their reports somewhat or lead them to judge their children more harshly (Hughes & Barad, 1983). Studies obtaining child self-reports and teacher reports could bolster what we know about the impact that violent families have on children.

The effects of SES on the prevalence and identification of family violence should also be considered in greater detail. Gelles (1987a) has noted that a large proportion of cases of family violence involve low-SES families. However, whether this statistic is indicative of a greater propensity of the impoverished to become violent within the family or due to their vulnerability to being identified by local child agencies as abusive is an important question.

Overlooked Topics

Studies examining child witnessing of violence typically combine visual and auditory modalities (e.g., Jaffe et al., 1986a). To our knowledge, these two groups have not been separated out for purposes of differentiation. Children who only hear family violence (e.g., overhearing parental arguments) could differ from children who also see aggression in the family. Conceivably, one form could more easily lead to certain problems and vice versa, and comparing these groups could help further delineate the impact of family violence on children and adolescents.

Another important area of family violence that has been somewhat neglected is the issue of emotional or psychological abuse. A few studies are beginning to emerge that examine this potentially important form of violence. However, we know relatively little about its impact on the family and on children and adolescents in particular.

Notably, violence perpetrated by females has generated relatively little interest (Ben-David, 1993). Violent criminal behaviors by females in the public domain are relatively rare (Daniel & Kashani, 1983); however, familial violence by females appears to be more common (Ben-David, 1993) and often appears to be prompted by children's externalizing behaviors (Jouriles & Norwood, 1995). A number of viable explanations for this occurrence exist. For example, children are likely to spend more time with female than male caregivers. Similarly, females tend to be responsible for the majority of child care. Thus the time that female caregivers spend with their children may tend to be more stressed. However, these hypotheses remain largely untested.

In addition, spousal abuse that is perpetrated by a woman against a man is almost completely undocumented in the literature, although it is gaining attention in the popular press. Part of the problem appears to be the fact that female violence is commonly comorbid with male spousal violence, which causes difficulty when trying to tease apart the aggressor and victim roles (Ben-David, 1993). Even in cases where the female initiates the aggression, self-defense tactics by the male may actually result in greater damage to the female than that experienced by the male (Ben-David, 1993). Additionally, both males and females indicate that they are more tolerant of female-to-male violence than male-to-female violence (Koski & Mangold, 1988). The effects that child witnessing of female-to-male abuse may have on youngsters are unclear.

Two other forms of family violence were examined in this book: sibling-on-sibling abuse and child witnessing of elder abuse. Some research suggests that sibling abuse is the most frequent type of abuse (e.g., Korbin, 1995). Nevertheless, reliable data regarding this problem are not available. For example, we do not know the extent of injury commonly suffered by children who are abused by their siblings. Typically, parents believe that sibling violence is, at least to a certain extent, normal. However, at what point do parents and children recognize it as a serious and potentially damaging problem? With regard to elder abuse, research is not available that explores the effects of children's observation of this form of familial violence. However, we can hypothesize on some of the negative impact it could have on children, such as providing a model of violence to them. This issue would seem particularly important given the increasingly aged nature of our population.

Finally, in families with multiple children, a child could witness a sibling abusing a parent (Dickstein, 1988). This problem is not reported much in the literature, but in our clinical work, we certainly have heard reports of this situation occurring. The impact of this violence on a child could include aggression, internalizing problems, or a loss of respect for the parent or sibling; regardless, these hypotheses await investigation by researchers.

REFERENCES

Achenbach, T. M. (1991). *Manual for the Child Behavior Checklist and Revised Child Behavior Profile.* Burlington, VT: University Associates in Psychiatry.

Adam, B. S., Everett, B. L., & O'Neal, E. (1992). PTSD in physically and sexually abused psychiatrically hospitalized children. *Child Psychiatry and Human Development, 23,* 3-8.

Adams, D., Overholser, J., & Lehnert, K. (1996, November). *Child abuse, family functioning and adolescent suicidal behavior.* Poster session presented at the annual meeting of the Association for the Advancement of Behavior Therapy, New York.

Allan, W. D., Kashani, J. H., Dahlmeier, J., Taghizadeh, P., & Reid, J. C. (in press). Psychometric properties and clinical utility of the Scale for Suicide Ideation with inpatient children. *Journal of Abnormal Child Psychology.*

Allan, W. D., Kashani, J. H., & Reid, J. C. (in press). Parental hostility: Impact on the family. *Child Psychiatry and Human Development.*

Allen, D. M., & Tarnowski, K. J. (1989). Depressive characteristics of physically abused children. *Journal of Abnormal Child Psychology, 17,* 1-11.

American Academy of Child and Adolescent Psychiatry. (1997). Practice parameters for the forensic evaluation of children and adolescents who may have been physically or sexually abused. *Journal of the American Academy of Child and Adolescent Psychiatry, 36,* 423-442.

American Psychiatric Association (APA). (1994). *Diagnostic and statistical manual of mental disorders* (4th ed.). Washington, DC: Author.

Appleton, W. (1980). The battered woman syndrome. *Annals of Emergency Medicine, 9,* 84-91.

Augoustinos, M. (1987). Developmental effects of child abuse: Recent findings. *Child Abuse & Neglect, 11,* 15-27.

Bachman, R., & Coker, A. L. (1995). Police involvement in domestic violence: The interactive effects of victim injury, offender's history of violence, and race. *Violence and Victims, 10,* 91-106.

Barnett, O. W., Fagan, R. W., & Booker, J. M. (1991). Hostility and stress as mediators of aggression in violent men. *Journal of Family Violence, 6,* 217-241.

Barth, R. P., Ash, J. R., & Hacking, S. (1986). Identifying, screening and engaging high-risk clients in private non-profit child abuse prevention programs. *Child Abuse & Neglect, 10,* 99-109.

Barton, K., & Baglio, C. (1993). The nature of stress in child-abusing families: A factor analytic study. *Psychological Reports, 73,* 1047-1055.

Baskett, L. M., & Johnson, S. M. (1982). The young child's interactions with parents versus siblings: A behavioral analysis. *Child Development, 53,* 643-650.

Beck, A. T., Kovacs, M., & Weissman, A. (1979). Assessment of suicidal intention: The Scale for Suicide Ideation. *Journal of Consulting and Clinical Psychology, 47,* 343-352.

Beck, A. T., Rush, A. J., Shaw, B. F., & Emery, G. (1979). *Cognitive therapy of depression.* New York: Guilford.

Beck, A., Weissman, A., Lester, D., & Trexler, L. (1974). The measurement of pessimism: The Hopelessness Scale. *Journal of Consulting and Clinical Psychology, 42,* 861-865.

Beck, C. M., & Ferguson, D. (1981). Aged abuse. *Journal of Gerontological Nursing, 7,* 333-336.

Bell, C. C., & Chance-Hill, G. (1991). Treatment of violent families. *Journal of the National Medical Association, 83,* 203-208.

Bell-Dolan, D., & Allan, W. D. (1997). *Assessing elementary school children's social skills: Evaluation of the parent version of the MESSY.* Manuscript submitted for publication.

Bell-Dolan, D., & Allan, W. D. (in press). Cognitive-behavioral approaches to assessment and treatment of childhood trauma. In S. Husain (Ed.), *Traumatized children: Lessons from Bosnia.* New York: Johns Hopkins University Press.

Ben-David, S. (1993). The two facets of female violence: The public and the domestic domains. *Journal of Family Violence, 8,* 345-359.

Bernstein, D. P., Ahluvalia, T., Pogge, D., & Handelsman, L. (1997). Validity of the Childhood Trauma Questionnaire in an adolescent psychiatric population. *Journal of the American Academy of Child and Adolescent Psychiatry, 36,* 340-348.

Bird, H. R., Yager, T. J., Staghezza, B., Gould, M. S., Canino, G., & Rubio-Stipec, M. (1990). Impairment in the epidemiological measurement of childhood psychopathology in the community. *Journal of the American Academy of Child and Adolescent Psychiatry, 29,* 796-803.

Black, D., Harris-Hendriks, J., & Kaplan, T. (1992). Father kills mother: Post-traumatic stress disorder in the children. *Psychotherapy and Psychosomatics, 57,* 152-157.

Black, D., & Kaplan, T. (1988). Father kills mother: Issues and problems encountered by a child psychiatric team. *British Journal of Psychiatry, 153,* 624-630.

Bottom, W., & Lancaster, J. (1981). An ecological orientation toward human abuse. *Family and Community Health, 4,* 1-10.

Brizer, D. A. (1988). Psychopharmacology and the management of violent patients. *Psychiatric Clinics of North America, 11,* 551-568.

Brosig, C. L., & Kalichman, S. C. (1992). Clinicians' reporting of suspected child abuse: A review of the empirical literature. *Clinical Psychology Review, 12,* 155-168.

Burman, S., & Allen-Meares, P. (1994). Neglected victims of murder: Children's witness to parental homicide. *Social Work, 39,* 28-34.

Burrowes, K. L., Hales, R. E., & Arrington, E. (1988). Research on the biologic aspects of violence. *Psychiatric Clinics of North America, 11,* 499-509.

Bushman, B. J., & Cooper, H. M. (1990). Effects of alcohol on human aggression: An integrative research review. *Psychological Bulletin, 107,* 341-354.

Cappell, C., & Heiner, R. B. (1990). The intergenerational transmission of family aggression. *Journal of Family Violence, 5,* 135-152.

Carlson, B. E. (1990). Adolescent observers of marital violence. *Journal of Family Violence, 5,* 285-299.

Cascardi, M., & O'Leary, K. G. (1992). Depressive symptomatology, self-esteem, and self-blame in battered women. *Journal of Family Violence, 7,* 249-259.

Chambers, W. J., Puig-Antich, J., Hirsch, M., Paez, P., Ambrosini, P. J., Tabrizi, M. A., & Davies, M. (1985). The assessment of affective disorders in children and adolescents by semistructured interview: Test-retest reliability for school age children, present episode version. *Archives of General Psychiatry, 42,* 696-702.

Cicchetti, D., Rogosch, F. A., Lynch, M., & Holt, K. D. (1993). Resilience in maltreated children: Processes leading to adaptive outcome. *Development and Psychopathology, 5,* 629-647.

Clarke, G., Lewinsohn, P., & Hops, H. (1990). *Leader's manual for adolescent groups: Adolescent coping with depression course.* Eugene, OR: Castalia.

Conners, C. K. (1985). *The Conners Rating Scales: Instruments for the assessment of childhood psychopathology.* Unpublished manuscript, Children's Hospital National Medical Center, Washington, DC.

Coopersmith, S. (1967). *The antecedents of self-esteem.* San Francisco: Freeman.

Costello, E. J., Edelbrock, C., & Costello, A. J. (1985). Validity of the NIMH Diagnostic Interview Schedule for Children: A comparison between psychiatric and pediatric referrals. *Journal of Abnormal Child Psychology, 13,* 579-595.

Cummings, E. M., Vogel, D., Cummings, J. S., & El-Sheikh, M. (1989). Children's responses to different forms of expression of anger between adults. *Child Development, 60,* 1392-1404.

Curtis, G. C. (1963). Violence breeds violence–perhaps? *American Journal of Psychiatry, 120,* 386-387.

Daniel, A. E., & Kashani, J. H. (1983). Women who commit crimes of violence. *Psychiatric Annals, 13,* 697-713.

Davis, K. E. (1988). Interparental violence: The children as victims. *Issues in Comprehensive Pediatric Nursing, 11,* 291-302.

Deblinger, E., McLeer, S. V., Atkins, M. S., Ralphe, D., & Foa, E. (1989). Post-traumatic stress in sexually abused, physically abused, and nonabused children. *Child Abuse and Neglect, 13,* 403-408.

Dickstein, L. J. (1988). Spouse abuse and other domestic violence. *Psychiatric Clinics of North America, 11,* 611-628.

Drake, V. K. (1982). Battered women: A health care problem in disguise. *Image, 14,* 40-47.

Dunn, J. (1988). Sibling influences on childhood development. *Journal of Child Psychology and Psychiatry and Allied Disciplines, 29,* 119-127.

Dutton, D. G. (1995a). Intimate abusiveness. *Clinical Psychology: Science and Practice, 2,* 207-224.

Dutton, D. G. (1995b). Male abusiveness in intimate relationships. *Clinical Psychology Review, 15,* 567-581.

Dutton, D. G., van Ginkel, C., & Starzomski, A. (1995). The role of shame and guilt in the intergenerational transmission of abusiveness. *Violence and Victims, 10,* 121-131.

Edelson, J. L., & Frank, M. D. (1991). Rural interventions in woman battering: One state's strategies. *Families in Society: The Journal of Contemporary Human Services, 72,* 543-551.

Edman, S. O., Cole, D. A., & Howard, G. S. (1990). Convergent and discriminant validity of FACES-III: Family adaptability and cohesion. *Family Process, 29,* 95-103.

Edmundson, S. E., & Collier, P. (1993). Child protection and emotional abuse: Definition, identification and usefulness within an educational setting. *Educational Psychology in Practice, 8,* 198-206.

Egeland, B., Jacobvitz, D., & Sroufe, L. A. (1988). Breaking the cycle of abuse. *Child Development, 59,* 1080-1088.

Elbow, M. (1982). Children of violent marriages: The forgotten victims. *Social Casework: The Journal of Contemporary Social Work, 63,* 465-471.

94   THE IMPACT OF FAMILY VIOLENCE ON CHILDREN

Elliott, F. A. (1982). Neurological findings in adult minimal brain dysfunction and the dyscontrol syndrome. *Journal of Nervous and Mental Disease, 170,* 680-687.

Emery, R. E. (1989). Family violence. *American Psychologist, 44,* 321-328.

Famularo, R., Fenton, T., & Kinscherff, R. (1993). Child maltreatment and the development of posttraumatic stress disorder. *American Journal of Diseases of Children, 147,* 755-760.

Famularo, R., Kinscherff, R., Bunshaft, D., Spivak, G., & Fenton, T. (1989). Parental compliance to court-ordered treatment interventions in cases of child maltreatment. *Child Abuse & Neglect, 13,* 507-514.

Famularo, R., Kinscherff, R., & Fenton, T. (1992). Psychiatric diagnoses of maltreated children: Preliminary findings. *Journal of the American Academy of Child and Adolescent Psychiatry, 31,* 863-867.

Fantuzzo, J. W., DePaola, L. M., Lambert, L., Martino, T., Anderson, G., & Sutton, S. (1991). Effects of interparental violence on the psychological adjustment and competencies of young children. *Journal of Consulting and Clinical Psychology, 59,* 258-265.

Feindler, E. L., & Becker, J. V. (1994). Interventions in family violence involving children and adolescents. In J. H. Gentry & P. Schlegel (Eds.), *Reason to hope: A psychosocial perspective on violence and youth* (pp. 405-430). Washington, DC: American Psychological Association.

Flemons, D. G. (1989). An ecosystemic view of family violence. *Family Therapy, 16,* 1-10.

Foster, S. L., & Robin, A. L. (1989). Parent-adolescent conflict. In E. J. Mash & R. A. Barkley (Eds.), *Treatment of childhood disorders* (pp. 493-528). New York: Guilford.

Garbarino, J. (1977). The human ecology of child maltreatment: A conceptual model for research. *Journal of Marriage and the Family, 39,* 721-735.

Gelles, R. J. (1987a). The family and its role in the abuse of children. *Psychiatric Annals, 17,* 229-232.

Gelles, R. J. (1987b). *Family violence.* Newbury Park, CA: Sage.

Gelles, R. J. (1989). Child abuse and violence in single-parent families: Parent absence and economic deprivation. *American Journal of Orthopsychiatry, 59,* 492-501.

Gelles, R. J., & Maynard, P. E. (1987). A structural family systems approach to intervention in cases of family violence. *Family Relations, 36,* 270-275.

Gelles, R., & Straus, M. (1979). Determinants of violence in the family: Toward a theoretical integration. In W. Burr (Ed.), *Theories about the family* (pp. 549-581). New York: Free Press.

Gentry, C. E., & Eaddy, V. B. (1980). Treatment of children in spouse abusive families. *Victimology: An International Journal, 5,* 240-250.

Gerbi, L. (1994). Spousal violence: Understanding and intervention techniques. *Journal of Family Psychotherapy, 5,* 19-31.

Gilbert, M. J. (1996, May-June). Society: We made it, we can change it. *American Academy of Child and Adolescent Psychiatry News,* p. 29.

Giller, B. (1990). All in the family: Violence in the Jewish home. *Women and Therapy, 10,* 101-109.

Glaser, B. A., Sayger, T. V., & Horne, A. M. (1993). Three types of Family Environment Scale profiles: Functional, distressed, and abusive families. *Journal of Family Violence, 8,* 303-311.

Goldman, E. L. (1994, November). Calling domestic violence by its name–disease. *Clinical Psychiatry News,* p. 5.

Green, A. H., Gaines, R. W., & Sandgrund, A. (1974). Child abuse: Pathological syndrome of family interaction. *American Journal of Psychiatry, 131,* 882-886.

Griffin, L. W., & Williams, O. J. (1992). Abuse among African-American elderly. *Journal of Family Violence, 7,* 19-35.

Grusznski, R. J., & Carrillo, T. P. (1988). Who completes a batterer's treatment group? An empirical investigation. *Journal of Family Violence, 3,* 141-150.

Gully, K. J., Dengerink, H. A., Pepping, M., & Bergstrom, D. (1981). Sibling contribution to violent behavior. *Journal of Marriage and the Family, 43,* 333-337.

Gunn, J., & Bonn, J. (1971). Criminality and violence in epileptic prisoners. *British Journal of Psychiatry, 118,* 337-343.

Harper, J. (1991). Children's play: The differential effects of intrafamilial physical and sexual abuse. *Child Abuse & Neglect, 15,* 89-98.

Havens, L. L. (1972). Youth, violence, and the nature of family life. *Psychiatric Annals, 2,* 18-29.

Henning, K., Leitenberg, H., Coffey, P., Turner, T., & Bennett, R. T. (1996). Long-term psychological and social impact of witnessing physical conflict between parents. *Journal of Interpersonal Violence, 11,* 35-51.

Herjanic, B., & Reich, W. (1982). Development of a structured psychiatric interview for children: Agreement between child and parent on individual symptoms. *Journal of Abnormal Child Psychology, 10,* 307-324.

Herrenkohl, E. C., Herrenkohl, R. C., Toedter, L., & Yanushefski, A. M. (1984). Parent-child interactions in abusive and nonabusive families. *Journal of the American Academy of Child Psychiatry, 23,* 641-648.

Herrenkohl, R. C., & Herrenkohl, E. C. (1981). Some antecedents and developmental consequences of child maltreatment. *New Directions for Child Development, 11,* 57-76.

Hershorn, M., & Rosenbaum, A. (1985). Children of marital violence: A closer look at the unintended victims. *American Journal of Orthopsychiatry, 55,* 260-266.

Hoffman-Plotkin, D., & Twentyman, C. T. (1984). A multimodal assessment of behavioral and cognitive deficits in abused and neglected preschoolers. *Child Development, 55,* 794-802.

Hollander, N. (1986). Homicides of abused children prematurely returned home. *Forensic Science International, 30,* 85-91.

Home, A. (1991-1992). Responding to domestic violence: A comparison of social workers' and police officers' interventions. *Social Work and Social Sciences Review, 3,* 150-162.

Howell, M. J., & Pugliesi, K. L. (1988). Husbands who harm: Predicting spousal violence by men. *Journal of Family Violence, 3,* 15-27.

Hughes, H. M. (1982). Brief interventions with children in a battered women's shelter: A model preventive program. *Family Relations, 31,* 495-502.

Hughes, H. M. (1988). Psychological and behavioral correlates of family violence in child witnesses and victims. *American Journal of Orthopsychiatry, 58,* 77-90.

Hughes, H. M., & Barad, S. J. (1983). Psychological functioning of children in a battered women's shelter: A preliminary investigation. *American Journal of Orthopsychiatry, 53,* 525-531.

Hurley, D. J., & Jaffe, P. (1990). Children's observations of violence: II. Clinical implications for children's mental health professionals. *Canadian Journal of Psychiatry, 35,* 471-476.

Husain, A., & Daniel, A. (1984). A comparative study of filicidal and abusive mothers. *Canadian Journal of Psychiatry, 29,* 596-598.

Jaffe, P. G., Hurley, D. J., & Wolfe, D. (1990). Children's observations of violence: I. Critical issues in child development and intervention planning. *Canadian Journal of Psychiatry, 35,* 466-470.

Jaffe, P., Wilson, S. K., & Wolfe, D. (1989). Specific assessment and intervention strategies for children exposed to wife battering: Preliminary empirical investigation. *Canadian Journal of Community Mental Health, 7,* 157-163.

Jaffe, P., Wolfe, D., Wilson, S., & Zak, L. (1986a). Similarities in behavioral and social maladjustment among child victims and witnesses to family violence. *American Journal of Orthopsychiatry, 56,* 142-146.

Jaffe, P., Wolfe, D., Wilson, S. K., & Zak, L. (1986b). Family violence and child adjustment: A comparative analysis of girls' and boys' behavioral symptoms. *American Journal of Psychiatry, 143,* 74-77.

Jalongo, M. R., & Renck, M. A. (1985). Sibling relationships: A recurrent developmental and literary theme. *Childhood Education, 61,* 346-351.

Johnson, D. G. (1979). Abuse and neglect–not for children only! *Journal of Gerontological Nursing, 5,* 11-13.

Jouriles, E. N., & Norwood, W. D. (1995). Physical aggression toward boys and girls in families characterized by the battering of women. *Journal of Family Psychology, 9,* 69-78.

Jurich, A. P. (1990). Families who physically abuse adolescents. In S. M. Stith, M. B. Williams, & K. H. Rosen (Eds.), *Violence hits home: Comprehensive treatment approaches to domestic violence* (pp. 126-150). New York: Springer.

Kalmuss, D. (1984). The intergenerational transmission of marital aggression. *Journal of Marriage and the Family, 46,* 11-19.

Kaplan, S. J., Pelcovitz, D., Salzinger, S., Mandel, F., & Weiner, M. (1997). Adolescent physical abuse and suicide attempts. *Journal of the American Academy of Child and Adolescent Psychiatry, 36,* 799-808.

Kashani, J. H., Daniel, A. E., Dandoy, A. C., & Holcomb, W. R. (1992). Family violence: Impact on children. *Journal of the American Academy of Child and Adolescent Psychiatry, 31,* 181-189.

Kashani, J. H., Daniel, A. E., Sulzberger, L. A., Rosenberg, T. K., & Reid, J. C. (1987). Conduct disordered adolescents from a community sample. *Canadian Journal of Psychiatry, 32,* 756-760.

Kashani, J. H., Darby, P. J., Allan, W. D., Hartke, K. L., & Reid, J. C. (1997). Intrafamilial homicide committed by juveniles: Examination of a sample with recommendations for prevention. *Journal of Forensic Sciences, 42,* 873-878.

Kashani, J. H., Mehregany, D., Allan, W. D., & Kelly, K. (in press). *The family guide to raising happy, well-adjusted children* [tentative title]. New York: Crown.

Kashani, J. H., & Ray, J. S. (1987). Major depression with delusional features in a preschool-age child. *Journal of the American Academy of Child and Adolescent Psychiatry, 26,* 110-112.

Kashani, J. H., Reid, J. C., & Rosenberg, T. K. (1989). Levels of hopelessness in children and adolescents: A developmental perspective. *Journal of Consulting and Clinical Psychology, 57,* 496-499.

Kashani, J. H., Rosenberg, T., Beck, N. C., Reid, J. C., & Battle, E. F. (1987). Characteristics of well adjusted adolescents. *Canadian Journal of Psychiatry, 32,* 418-422.

Kashani, J. H., Shekim, W. O., Burk, J. P., & Beck, N. C. (1987). Abuse as a predictor of psychopathology in children and adolescents. *Journal of Clinical Child Psychology, 16,* 43-50.

Kashani, J. H., & Shepherd, J. A. (1990). Aggression in adolescents: The role of social support and personality. *Canadian Journal of Psychiatry, 35,* 311-315.

Katsikas, S., Petretic-Jackson, P., & Knowles, E. (1996, November). *Long-term sequelae of childhood maltreatment: An attachment theory perspective.* Poster session presented at the annual meeting of the Association for the Advancement of Behavior Therapy, New York.

Kaufman, A. S., & Kaufman, N. L. (1983). *The Kaufman Assessment Battery for Children.* Circle Pines, MN: American Guidance Service.

Kaufman, J., & Zigler, E. (1987). Do abused children become abusive parents? *American Journal of Orthopsychiatry, 57,* 186-192.

Kazdin, A. E., French, N. H., Unis, A. S., Esveldt-Dawson, K., & Sherick, R. B. (1983). Hopelessness, depression, and suicidal intent among psychiatrically disturbed inpatient children. *Journal of Consulting and Clinical Psychology, 51,* 504-510.

Kazdin, A. E., Moser, J., Colbus, D., & Bell, R. (1985). Depressive symptoms among physically abused and psychiatrically disturbed children. *Journal of Abnormal Psychology, 94,* 298-307.

Kazdin, A. E., Rodgers, A., & Colbus, D. (1986). The Hopelessness Scale for Children: Psychometric characteristics and concurrent validity. *Journal of Consulting and Clinical Psychology, 54,* 241-245.

Kempe, C. H., Silverman, F. N., Steele, B. F., Droegemueller, W., & Silver, H. K. (1962). The battered-child syndrome. *Journal of the American Medical Association, 181,* 17-24.

Kilpatrick, A. C., & Lockhart, L. L. (1991). Studying sensitive family issues: Problems and possibilities for practitioners. *Families in Society: The Journal of Contemporary Human Services, 72,* 610-617.

Klerman, L. V. (1993). The relationship between adolescent parenthood and inadequate parenting. *Children and Youth Services, 15,* 309-320.

Korbin, J. E. (1995). Social networks and family violence in cross-cultural perspective. In G. B. Melton (Ed.), *The individual, the family, and social good: Personal fulfillment in times of change* (pp. 107-134). Lincoln: University of Nebraska Press.

Kornblit, A. L. (1994). Domestic violence: An emerging health issue. *Social Science and Medicine, 39,* 1181-1188.

Kosberg, J. I. (1988). Preventing elder abuse: Identification of high risk factors prior to placement decisions. *Gerontologist, 28,* 43-50.

Koski, P. R., & Mangold, W. D. (1988). Gender effects in attitudes about family violence. *Journal of Family Violence, 3,* 225-237.

Kovacs, M. (1992). *Children's Depression Inventory: CDI manual.* North Tonawanda, NY: Multi-Health Systems.

Kreuz, L. E., & Rose, R. M. (1972). Assessment of aggressive behavior and plasma testosterone in a young criminal population. *Psychosomatic Medicine, 34,* 321-332.

Krugman, R. D. (1983-1985). Fatal child abuse: Analysis of 24 cases. *Pediatrician, 12,* 68-72.

Larrance, D. T., & Twentyman, C. T. (1983). Maternal attributions and child abuse. *Journal of Abnormal Psychology, 92,* 449-457.

Levinson, D. (1989). *Family violence in cross-cultural perspective.* Newbury Park, CA: Sage.

Lewis, D. O., Lovely, R., Yeager, C., & Femina, D. D. (1989). Toward a theory of the genesis of violence: A follow-up study of delinquents. *Journal of the American Academy of Child and Adolescent Psychiatry, 28,* 431-436.

Lipovsky, J. A. (1991). Posttraumatic stress disorder in children. *Family and Community Health, 14,* 42-51.

Lovell, M. L., & Richey, C. A. (1991). Implementing agency-based social-support skill training. *Families in Society: The Journal of Contemporary Human Services, 72,* 563-572.

Main, M., & George, C. (1985). Responses of abused and disadvantaged toddlers to distress in agemates: A study in the day care setting. *Developmental Psychology, 21,* 407-412.

Maiuro, R. D., Cahn, T. S., Vitaliano, P. P., Wagner, B. C., & Zegree, J. B. (1988). Anger, hostility, and depression in domestically violent versus generally assaultive men and nonviolent control subjects. *Journal of Consulting and Clinical Psychology, 56,* 17-23.

Malkin, C. M., & Lamb, M. E. (1994). Child maltreatment: A test of sociobiological theory. *Journal of Comparative Family Studies, 25,* 121-133.

March, J. S., Parker, J. D. A., Sullivan, K., Stallings, P., & Conners, C. K. (1997). The Multidimensional Anxiety Scale for Children (MASC): Factor structure, reliability, and validity. *Journal of the American Academy of Child and Adolescent Psychiatry, 36,* 554-565.

Matson, J. L. (1990). *Matson Evaluation of Social Skills With Youngsters: Manual.* Orland Park, IL: International Diagnostic Systems.

Mattsson, A., Schalling, D., Olweus, D., Low, H., & Svensson, J. (1980). Plasma testosterone, aggressive behavior, and personality dimensions in young male delinquents. *Journal of the American Academy of Child Psychiatry, 19,* 476-490.

McCloskey, L. A., Figueredo, A. J., & Koss, M. P. (1995). The effects of systemic family violence on children's mental health. *Child Development, 66,* 1239-1261.

Meloy, J. R. (1996). Stalking (obsessional following): A review of some preliminary studies. *Aggression and Violent Behavior, 1,* 147-162.

Meloy, J. R., & Gothard, S. (1995). Demographic and clinical comparison of obsessional followers and offenders with mental disorders. *American Journal of Psychiatry, 152,* 258-263.

Miller, T. W., & Veltkamp, L. J. (1995). Clinical and preventive issues in child custody disputes. *Child Psychiatry and Human Development, 25,* 267-280.

Milner, J. S., Robertson, K. R., & Rogers, D. L. (1990). Childhood history of abuse and adult child abuse potential. *Journal of Family Violence, 5,* 15-34.

Mohr, J. W., & McKnight, C. K. (1971). Violence as a function of age and relationship with special reference to matricide. *Canadian Psychiatric Association Journal, 16,* 29-32.

Monahan, J. (1996). Violence prediction: The past twenty and the next twenty years. *Criminal Justice and Behavior, 23,* 107-120.

Monahan, J., & Arnold, J. (1996). Violence by people with mental illness: A consensus statement by advocates and researchers. *Psychiatric Rehabilitation Journal, 19,* 67-70.

Moore, J. G. (1975). Yo-yo children: Victims of matrimonial violence. *Child Welfare, 54,* 557-566.

Moos, R. H., & Moos, B. S. (1984). *Family Environment Scale manual.* Palo Alto, CA: Consulting Psychologists.

Mufson, L., Moreau, D., Weissman, M. M., & Klerman, G. L. (1993). *Interpersonal psychotherapy for depressed adolescents.* New York: Guilford.

Murdoch, D., Pihl, R. O., & Ross, D. (1990). Alcohol and crimes of violence: Present issues. *International Journal of the Addictions, 25,* 1065-1081.

Myers, S. A. (1970). Maternal filicide. *American Journal of Diseases of Children, 120,* 534-536.

Neighbors, B., Forehand, R., & McVicar, D. (1993). Resilient adolescents and interparental conflict. *American Journal of Orthopsychiatry, 63,* 462-471.

Nesbit, W. C., & Karagianis, L. D. (1987). Psychological abuse in the home and in the school. *Canadian Journal of Education, 12,* 177-183.

Neubauer, P. B. (1983). The importance of the sibling experience. *Psychoanalytic Study of the Child, 38,* 325-336.

Newberger, E. H. (1991). Child abuse. In M. L. Rosenberg & M. A. Fenley (Eds.), *Violence in America: A public health approach.* New York: Oxford University Press.

Newberger, E. H., Hampton, R. I., Marx, T. J., & White, K. M. (1986). Child abuse and pediatric social illness: An epidemiological analysis and ecological reformulation. *American Journal of Orthopsychiatry, 56,* 589-601.

Nielson, J., Christensen, A.-L., Schultz-Larsen, J., & Yde, H. (1973). A psychiatric-psychological study of patients with the XYY syndrome found outside of institutions. *Acta Psychiatrica Scandinavica, 49,* 159-168.

Nightingale, N. N., & Walker, E. F. (1991). The impact of social class and parental maltreatment on the cognitive functioning of children. *Journal of Family Violence, 6,* 115-130.

O'Leary, K. D., & Jouriles, E. N. (1994). Psychological abuse between adult partners: Prevalence and impact on partners and children. In L. L'Abate (Ed.), *Handbook of developmental family psychology and psychopathology* (pp. 330-340). New York: John Wiley.

Ollendick, T. H. (1983). Reliability and validity of the Revised Fear Survey Schedule for Children. *Behaviour Research and Therapy, 21,* 685-692.

Olson, D. H. (1986). Circumplex model VII: Validation studies and FACES III. *Family Process, 25,* 337-351.

Olson, D. H., Russell, C. S., & Sprenkle, D. H. (1983). Circumplex model of marital and family systems: VI. Theoretical update. *Family Process, 22,* 69-83.

Osuna, E., Ceron, M., Banon, R., & Luna, A. (1995). Violence in the family setting: An analysis of mistreatment of minors and women. *Medicine and Law, 14,* 117-122.

Patterson, G. R. (1984). Siblings: Fellow travellers in coercive family processes. *Advances in the Study of Aggression, 1,* 174-215.

Pelcovitz, D., Kaplan, S., Goldenberg, B., Mandel, F., Lehane, J., & Guarrera, J. (1994). Post-traumatic stress disorder in physically abused adolescents. *Journal of the American Academy of Child and Adolescent Psychiatry, 33,* 305-312.

Peled, E., & Davis, D. (1995). *Groupwork with children of battered women: A practitioner's guide.* Thousand Oaks, CA: Sage.

Perrin, S., & Last, C. G. (1992). Do childhood anxiety measures measure anxiety? *Journal of Abnormal Child Psychology, 20,* 567-578.

Pfeffer, C. R. (1996, November-December). Violence in America: A critical concern for child and adolescent psychiatrist. *American Academy of Child and Adolescent News,* pp. 19-22.

Pillemer, K., & Finkelhor, D. (1989). Causes of elder abuse: Caregiver stress versus problem relatives. *American Journal of Orthopsychiatry, 59,* 179-187.

Porter, B., & O'Leary, D. (1980). Marital discord and childhood behavior problems. *Journal of Abnormal Child Psychology, 8,* 287-295.

Post, S. (1982). Adolescent parricide in abusive families. *Child Welfare, 61,* 445-455.

Poznanski, E., Cook, S., & Carroll, B. (1979). A depression rating scale for children. *Pediatrics, 64,* 442-450.

Preston, G. (1986). The post-separation family and the emotional abuse of children: An ecological approach. *Australian Journal of Sex, Marriage, and the Family, 7,* 40-49.

Pynoos, R. S., & Nader, K. (1990). Children's exposure to violence and traumatic death. *Psychiatric Annals, 20,* 334-344.

Quay, H. C., & Peterson, D. R. (1975). *Manual for the Behavior Problem Checklist.* Unpublished manuscript.

Radbill, S. X. (1974). A history of child abuse and infanticide. In R. E. Helfer & C. H. Kempe (Eds.), *The battered child* (2nd ed., pp. 3-21). Chicago: University of Chicago Press.

Raine, A., Brennan, P., & Mednick, S. A. (1994). Birth complications combined with early maternal rejection at age 1 year predispose to violence crime at age 18 years. *Archives of General Psychiatry, 51,* 984-988.

Raine, A., Brennan, P., Mednick, B., & Mednick, S. A. (1996). High rates of violence, crime, academic problems, and behavioral problems in males with both early neuromotor deficits and unstable family environments. *Archives of General Psychiatry, 53,* 544-549.

Raine, A., Buchsbaum, M. S., Stanley, J., Lottenberg, S., Abel, L., & Stoddard, J. (1994). Selective reductions in prefrontal glucose metabolism in murderers. *Biological Psychiatry, 36,* 365-373.

Raine, A., Venables, P. H., & Williams, M. (1990). Relationships between central and autonomic measures of arousal at age 15 years and criminality at age 24 years. *Archives of General Psychiatry, 47,* 1003-1007.

Reichert, E. (1991). Perceptions of domestic violence against women: A cross-cultural survey of international students. *Response to the Victimization of Women and Children: Journal of the Center for Women Policy Studies, 14,* 13-18.

Reynolds, C. R., & Paget, K. D. (1981). Factor analysis of the Revised Children's Manifest Anxiety Scale for blacks, males, and females with a national normative sample. *Journal of Consulting and Clinical Psychology, 49,* 352-359.

Reynolds, C. R., & Paget, K. D. (1983). National normative and reliability data for the Revised Children's Manifest Anxiety Scale. *School Psychology Review, 12,* 324-336.

Reynolds, C. R., & Richmond, B. O. (1978). What I think and feel: A revised measure of children's manifest anxiety. *Journal of Abnormal Child Psychology, 6,* 271-280.

Richman, N., Stevenson, J., & Graham, P. (1982). *Pre-school to school: A behavioral study.* London: Academic Press.

Robinson, C. A., Wright, L. M., & Watson, W. L. (1994). A nontraditional approach to family violence. *Archives of Psychiatric Nursing, 8,* 30-37.

Rosenbaum, A., & O'Leary, K. D. (1981a). Marital violence: Characteristics of abusive couples. *Journal of Consulting and Clinical Psychology, 49,* 63-71.

Rosenbaum, A., & O'Leary, K. D. (1981b). Children: The unintended victims of marital violence. *American Journal of Orthopsychiatry, 51,* 692-699.

Ryan, M. A. (1995). Clinical ethics and intervention in domestic violence. *Ethics and Behavior, 5,* 279-282.

Rynerson, B. C., & Fishel, A. H. (1993). Domestic violence prevention training: Participant characteristics and treatment outcomes. *Journal of Family Violence, 8,* 253-266.

Sack, W. H., Mason, R., & Higgins, J. E. (1985). The single-parent family and abusive child punishment. *American Journal of Orthopsychiatry, 55,* 252-259.

Salzinger, S., Feldman, R. S., & Hammer, M. (1993). The effects of physical abuse on children's social relationships. *Child Development, 64,* 169-187.

Sandgrund, A., Gaines, R. W., & Green, A. H. (1974). Child abuse and mental retardation: A problem of cause and effect. *American Journal of Mental Deficiency, 79,* 327-330.

Saunders, D. G. (1996). Interventions for men who batter: Do we know what works? *Session: Psychotherapy in Practice, 2,* 81-93.

Schiavi, P. C., Theilgaard, A., Owen, D., & White, D. (1984). Sex chromosome anomalies, hormones, and aggressivity. *Archives of General Psychiatry, 41,* 93-99.

Schmitt, B. D. (1987). Seven deadly sins of childhood: Advising parents about difficult developmental phases. *Child Abuse & Neglect, 11,* 421-432.

Schotte, D. E., & Clum, G. A. (1982). Suicide ideation in a college population: A test of a model. *Journal of Consulting and Clinical Psychology, 50,* 690-696.

Seligman, M. E. P. (1975). *Helplessness: On depression, development, and death.* San Francisco: Freeman.

Shaffer, D., Gould, M. S., Brasic, J., Ambrosini, P., Fisher, P., Bird, H., & Aluwahlia, S. (1983). A Children's Global Assessment Scale (CGAS). *Archives of General Psychiatry, 40,* 1228-1231.

Silverman, W. K., & Eisen, A. R. (1992). Age differences in the reliability of parent and child reports of child anxious symptomatology using a structured interview. *Journal of the American Academy of Child and Adolescent Psychiatry, 31,* 117-124.

Silverman, W. K., & Nelles, W. B. (1988). The Anxiety Disorders Interview Schedule for Children. *Journal of the American Academy of Child and Adolescent Psychiatry, 27,* 772-778.

Sonnenberg, S. M. (1988). Victims of violence and post-traumatic stress disorder. *Psychiatric Clinics of North America, 11,* 581-590.

Spielberger, C. D. (1973). *Manual for the State-Trait Anxiety Inventory for Children.* Palo Alto, CA: Consulting Psychologists Press.

Stagg, V., Wills, G. D., & Howell, M. (1989). Psychopathology in early childhood witnesses of family violence. *Topics in Early Childhood Special Education, 9,* 73-87.

Starr, R. H. (1979). Child abuse. *American Psychologist, 34,* 872-878.

Steer, R. A., Kumar, G., & Beck, A. T. (1993). Self-reported suicidal ideation in adolescent psychiatric inpatients. *Journal of Consulting and Clinical Psychology, 61,* 1096-1099.

Stith, S. M., & Farley, S. C. (1993). A predictive model of male spousal violence. *Journal of Family Violence, 8,* 183-201.

Stone, L. A. (1996). The violence epidemic: Protecting our children and our futures. *The Developmentor: The Resident and Medical Student Newsletter of the American Academy of Child and Adolescent Psychiatry, 3,* 1-2.

Straus, M. A. (1979). Measuring intrafamily conflict and violence: The Conflict Tactics (CT) Scales. *Journal of Marriage and the Family, 41,* 75-88.

Straus, M. A., Gelles, R. J., & Steinmetz, S. K. (1980). *Behind closed doors: Violence in the American family.* New York: Doubleday/Anchor.

Suh, E. K., & Abel, E. M. (1990). The impact of spousal violence on the children of the abused. *Journal of Independent Social Work, 4,* 27-34.

Syers, M., & Edelson, J. L. (1992). The combined effects of coordinated criminal justice intervention in woman abuse. *Journal of Interpersonal Violence, 7,* 490-502.

Thoennes, N., Salem, P., & Pearson, J. (1995). Mediation and domestic violence: Current policies and practices. *Family and Conciliation Courts Review, 33,* 6-29.

Thorndike, R. L., Hagen, E. P., & Sattler, J. M. (1986). *Technical manual, Stanford-Binet Intelligence Scale* (4th ed.). Chicago: Riverside.

Tilden, V. P., Schmidt, T. A., Limandri, B. J., Chiodo, G. T., Garland, M. J., & Loveless, P. A. (1994). Factors that influence clinicians' assessment and management of family violence. *American Journal of Public Health, 84,* 628-633.

Tilden, V. P., & Shepherd, P. (1987). Battered women: The shadow side of families. *Holistic Nursing Practice, 1,* 25-32.

Turkel, S. B. (1996, June). Violence: Impact on children and adolescents. *American Academy of Child and Adolescent Psychiatry News,* pp. 21-23.

Valentine, L., & Feinauer, L. L. (1993). Resilience factors associated with female survivors of childhood sexual abuse. *American Journal of Family Therapy, 21,* 216-224.

van Dalen, A., & Glasserman, M. (1997). My father, Frankenstein: A child's view of battering parents. *Journal of the American Academy of Child and Adolescent Psychiatry, 36,* 1005-1007.

Walker, L. E. (1979). *The battered woman.* New York: Harper & Row.

Watt, N. F., David, J. P., Ladd, K. L., & Shamos, S. (1995). The life course of psychological resilience: A phenomenological perspective on deflecting life's slings and arrows. *Journal of Primary Prevention, 15,* 209-246.

Wechsler, D. (1967). *Manual for the Wechsler Preschool and Primary Scale of Intelligence.* San Antonio, TX: Psychological Corporation.

Wechsler, D. (1991). *Manual for the Wechsler Intelligence Scale for Children–III.* San Antonio, TX: Psychological Corporation.

Wetzel, L., & Ross, M. A. (1983). Psychological and social ramifications of battering: Observations leading to a counseling methodology for victims of domestic violence. *Personnel and Guidance Journal, 61,* 423-428.

Widom, C. S. (1989). The cycle of violence. *Science, 244,* 160-166.

Willbach, D. (1989). Ethics and family therapy: The case management of family violence. *Journal of Marital and Family Therapy, 15,* 43-52.

Wilson, M. I., Daly, M., & Weghorst, S. J. (1980). Household composition and the risk of child abuse and neglect. *Journal of Biosocial Science, 12,* 333-340.

Wilson, S. K., Cameron, S., Jaffe, P., & Wolfe, D. (1989). Children exposed to wife abuse: An intervention model. *Social Casework: The Journal of Contemporary Social Work, 70,* 180-184.

Wissow, L. S., Wilson, M. E. H., Roter, D., Larson, S., & Berman, H. I. (1992). Family violence and the evaluation of behavioral concerns in a pediatric primary care clinic. *Medical Care, 30*(suppl.), MS150-MS165.

Wolfe, D. A., & Bourdeau, P. A. (1987). Current issues in the assessment of abusive and neglectful parent-child relationships. *Behavioral Assessment, 9,* 271-290.

Wolfe, D. A., & Jaffe, P. (1991). Child abuse and family violence as determinants of child psychopathology. *Canadian Journal of Behavioural Science, 23,* 282-299.

Wolfe, D. A., Jaffe, P., Wilson, S. K., & Zak, L. (1985). Children of battered women: The relation of child behavior to family violence and maternal stress. *Journal of Consulting and Clinical Psychology, 53,* 657-665.

Wolfe, D. A., Sandler, J., & Kaufman, K. (1981). A competency-based parent training program for child abusers. *Journal of Consulting and Clinical Psychology, 49,* 633-640.

Wolfe, D. A., Zak, L., Wilson, S., & Jaffe, P. (1986). Child witnesses to violence between parents: Critical issues in behavioral and social adjustment. *Journal of Abnormal Child Psychology, 14,* 95-104.

Wright, S. A. (1994). Physical and emotional abuse and neglect of preschool children: A literature review. *Australian Occupational Therapy Journal, 41,* 55-63.

Yates, A. (1982). Legal issues in psychological abuse of children. *Clinical Pediatrics, 21,* 587-590.

Yegidis, B. L. (1992). Family violence: Contemporary research findings and practice issues. *Community Mental Health Journal, 28,* 519-530.

Yudofsky, S. C., Silver, J. M., & Hales, R. E. (1995). Treatment of aggressive disorders. In A. F. Schatzberg & C. B. Nemeroff (Eds.), *The American psychiatric press textbook of psychopharmacology* (pp. 735-751). Washington, DC: American Psychiatric Press.

Yule, W., & Canterbury, R. (1994). The treatment of post traumatic stress disorder in children and adolescents. *International Review of Psychiatry, 6,* 141-151.

INDEX

Abel, E.M., 35
Abreaction, 72
Abuse. *See* Family Violence
Achenbach, T.M., 23, 37, 59, 62
Adam, B.S., 27
Adams, D., 26
Adolescent Coping with Depression Course, 73
Ahluvalia, T., 57
Allan, W.D., 30, 31, 48, 61, 62, 72
Allen, D.M., 24, 25, 26
Allen-Meares, P., 40
American Academy of Child and Adolescent Psychiatry, 63
Antisocial personality disorder (ASPD), 14, *See also* Parental personality factors and psychiatric disorders
Anxiety, 26-27, 38, *See also* Post-traumatic stress disorder
Anxiety Disorders Interview Schedule for Children, 59
Appleton, W., 11, 13, 33
Arnold, J., 16
Arrington, E., 6
Ash, J.R., 82
Assessment
    child witnessing of family violence, 57-58
    degree of child abuse, 57
    family assessment, 62-63
    general child strategies, 56
    impact of family violence, 58-62
    validation of abuse, 63
Atkins, M.S., 27
Attachment. *See* Parent-child attachment

Augoustinos, M., 19, 21, 22
Bachman, R., 66
Baglio, C., 11
Banon, R., 5
Barad, S.J., 37, 38, 44, 88
Barnett, O.W., 15
Barth, R.P., 82
Barton, K., 11
Baskett, L.M., 30
Battered-child syndrome, 4
Battered woman syndrome. *See* Spousal violence
Battle, E.F., 71
Beck, A.T., 38, 61
Beck, C.M., 41, 42
Beck, N.C., 18, 19, 24, 71
Becker, J.V., 83
Behavioral management training, 69
Behavior Problem Checklist, 59
Bell, C.C., 77-78
Bell, R., 25
Bell-Dolan, D., 62, 72
Ben-David, S., 89
Bennett, R. T., 34
Bergstrom, D., 30
Berman, H.I., 62
Bernstein, D.P., 57
Biological perspective, 6-7
Bird, H.R., 58
Black, D., 40, 41
Bonn, J., 6
Booker, J.M., 15
Bottom, W., 11, 12
Bourdeau, P.A., 28, 58, 60, 62, 77
Brennan, P., 7

Brizer, D.A., 70
Brosig, C.L., 65, 66, 70
Buchsbaum, M.S., 6
Bunshaft, D., 67
Burk, J.P., 18, 19, 24
Burman, S., 40
Burrowes, K.L., 6, 7, 69
Bushman, B.J., 14
Cahn, T.S., 15
Cameron, S., 74
Canterbury, R., 72
Cappel, C., 8
Caregiver stress, 43
Carlson, B.E., 36, 37, 38, 40
Carrillo, T.P., 67, 69
Carroll, B., 61
Cascardi, M., 38
CBCL. See Child Behavior Checklist
CDI. See Children's Depression Inventory
Ceron, M., 5
CGAS. See Children's Global Assessment
    Scale
Chance-Hill, G., 77-78
Child Abuse Potential Inventory, 9
Child Behavior Checklist, 13, 37, 38, 59, 62,
    64
Child development, 19, 68, 82
Child homicide, 20, 52
Childhood Trauma Questionnaire, 57
Children's Depression Inventory, 25, 60, 64
Children's Depression Rating Scale, 61
Children's Global Assessment Scale
    (CGAS), 58
Children's play, 30, See also Social
    development
Child temperament, 11
Child Witness to Violence Interview, 58
Christensen, A.-L., 6
Cicchetti, D., 82
Clarke, G., 73
Clum, G.A., 61
Coffey, P., 34
Cognitive-behavioral therapy, 72, 73
Cognitive functioning
    assessment of, 61
    family violence effects on, 21-22
Coker, A.L., 66
Colbus, D., 25, 61

Cole, D.A., 63
Communication patterns, 12, 13
Communication training, 79-80
Conference on Equality, Development, and
    Peace, 51
Conflict Tactics Scale, 22, 62
Conners, C.K., 59, 60
Conners Parent's Rating Scale, 59
Conversion reaction, 31
Cook, S., 61
Cooper, H.M., 14
Coopersmith, S., 25
Corporal punishment, 27, 52, 69
Costello, A.J., 59
Costello, E.J., 59
Cross-cultural approach
    patterns, 50-52
    perceived effects of violence, 53
    societies without violence, 54, 83
    violence directed toward children, 52
    violence directed toward elders, 53, See
        also Elder abuse
    violence directed toward spouses, 52, See
        also Spousal violence
Cummings, E.M., 37
Cummings, J.S., 37
Curtis, G.C., 8
Cycle of abuse. See Intergenerational
    transmission
Dahlmeier, J., 61
Daly, M., 13
Dandoy, A.C., xi
Daniel, A.E., xi, 3, 10, 13, 14, 20, 23, 35, 89
Darby, P.J., 31, 39, 84
Darwin, Charles, 7
David, J.P., 81
Davis, D., 74
Davis, K.E., 34, 36, 88
Deblinger, E., 27
Dengerink, H.A., 30
Depression, See also Internalizing problems
    cause of family violence, 15
    result of family violence, 24-26
    treating, 72-73
Diagnostic Interview for Children and
    Adolescents (DICA), 59
Diagnostic Interview Schedule for Children
    and Adolescents (DISC), 59

Dickstein, L.J., 33, 90
Difficult developmental periods, 11, 68
Drake, V.K., 33, 34
Droegemueller, W., 4
Dunn, J., 30
Dutton, D.G., 8, 13, 15, 16, 35
Eaddy, V.B., 67, 68, 70, 71, 76, 77, 78, 79
Economic hardship. See Single parenthood
Edelbrock, C., 59
Edelson, J.L., 66, 84
Edman, S.O., 63
Egeland, B., 68, 71
Eisen, A.R., 60
Elbow, M., 36
Elder abuse
    definition of, 41
    etiology of, 42-43
    impact on children, 43-44
    prevalence of, 42-43
Elliott, F.A., 6, 7
El-Sheikh, M., 37
Emery, G., 38
Emery, R.E., 3, 19, 87
Emotional abuse. See Psychological
    maltreatment
Esveldt-Dawson, K., 25
Everett, B.L., 27
Externalizing Problems, 22-24, 37, 59
Fagan, R.W., 15
Familial stress, 11, 15, 24, 47
Family Adaptability and Cohesion Scale III
    (FACES-III), 63
Family Environment Scale (FES), 62-63
Family systems approaches, 10-13, 77-78
Family violence
    costs of, 5
    definition of, 2-4, 19
    nature of, 4
Famularo, R., 19, 22, 24, 27, 67
Fantuzzo, J.W., 37, 38, 39, 44, 49
Farley, S.C., 14
Federal Child Abuse Prevention and
    Treatment Act (PL93-237), 2, 18
Feinauer, L.L., 81
Feindler, E.L., 83
Feldman, R.S., 29
Femina, D.D., 9
Feminist movement, 34

Fenton, T., 19, 27, 67
Ferguson, D., 41, 42
Figueredo, A.J., 35
Finkelhor, D., 41, 42, 43
Fishel, A. H., 9
Flemons, D. G., 11
Foa, E., 27
Forehand, R., 82
Foster, S.L., 79
Frank, M.D., 66, 84
French, N. H., 25
Gaines, R. W., 11, 21
Garbarino, J., 8, 30, 51
Gelles, R.J., 3, 10, 11, 12, 13, 14, 16, 17, 18,
    66, 70, 77, 89
Gender, 44-45
Gentry, C.E., 67, 68, 70, 71, 76, 77, 78, 79
George, C., 28
Gerbi, L., 67, 68, 78, 79
Gilbert, M.J., 83
Giller, B., 70, 78, 79
Glaser, B.A., 62
Glasserman, M., 70
Goldman, E.L., 86
Gothard, S., 15
Graham, P., 31
Green, A.H., 11, 12, 16, 21
Grief. See Pathological bereavement
Griffin, L.W., 9, 43
Grusznski, R.J., 67, 69
Gully, K.J., 30
Gunn, J., 6
Hacking, S., 82
Hagen, E.P., 61
Hales, R.E., 6
Hammer, M., 29
Hampton, R.I., 3
Handelsman, L., 57
Harper, J., 30
Harris-Hendriks, J., 40
Hartke, K.L., 31
Havens, L.L., 4
Heiner, R.B., 8
Henning, K., 34, 39
Herjanic, B., 59
Herrenkohl, E.C., 20, 28
Herrenkohl, R.C., 20, 28
Hershorn, M., 36

Higgins, J.E., 12
Hoffman-Plotkin, D., 21, 23
Holcomb, W. R., xi
Hollander, N., 20
Holt, K.D., 82
Home, A., 66
Hopelessness Scale for Children, 25, 61
Hops, H., 73
Horne, A.M., 62
Howard, G.S., 63
Howell, M.J., 11, 37
Hughes, H.M., 36, 37, 38, 44, 70, 88
Hunter-gatherer societies, 54, See also
   Cross-cultural approach
Hurley, D.J., 11, 65, 73, 74
Husain, A., 20
Iceberg phenomenon, 5
Infanticide. See Child homicide
Insularity of families, 8, 29, 51, 85
Intergenerational transmission, 8-10, 11, 17,
   29, 43, 68, 70, 76, 84
Internalizing problems, 24-28, 37-39, 59-61
Interpersonal therapy, 73
Intervention strategies
   anger management, 67, 69
   biological interventions, 69-70, 72, 73
   family therapy, 2, 76-80
   legal responses, 66-67
   mediation, 66-67
   treatment of the child, 70-76
   treatment of the perpetrator, 67-70
Intrafamilial homicide, 38-39, 84-85 See
   also Lockage phenomenon
Jacobvitz, D., 68
Jaffe, P., 11, 17, 19, 22, 24, 28, 36, 37, 38,
   39, 58, 65, 73, 74, 76, 86, 89
Jalongo, M.R., 30
Johnson, D.G., 28, 42, 43
Johnson, S.M., 30
Jouriles, E.N., 47, 48, 89
Jurich, A. P., 11, 14, 18, 27, 47, 65, 67, 68,
   77, 80
Kalichman, S.C., 65, 66, 70
Kalmuss, D., 9
Kaplan, S. J., 26
Kaplan, T., 40, 41
Karagianis, L.D., 46, 49, 84

Kashani, J.H., xi, 3, 4, 6, 10, 13, 14, 18, 19,
   23, 24, 25, 26, 30, 31, 33, 34, 35, 36,
   39, 42, 43, 44, 48, 61, 71, 81, 84, 87,
   89
Katsikas, S., 28, 82
Kaufman Assessment Battery for Children
   (K-ABC), 61
Kaufman, A.S., 61
Kaufman, J., 10
Kaufman, K., 69
Kaufman, N.L., 61
Kazdin, A.E., 25, 61
Kelly, K., 30
Kempe, C.H., 4, 10
Kilpatrick, A.C., 18, 88
Kinscherff, R., 19, 27, 67
Klerman, G.L., 73
Klerman, L.V., 3, 13, 83
Knowles, E., 28
Korbin, J.E., 51, 52, 53, 54, 89
Kornblit, A.L., 31
Kosberg, J.I., 43
Koski, P.R., 89
Koss, M.P., 35
Kovacs, M., 25, 60, 61, 64
Kreuz, L.E., 7
Krugman, R. D., 20
Kumar, G., 61
Ladd, K.L., 81
Lamb, M. E., 8
Lancaster, J., 11, 12
Larrance, D.T., 15
Larson, S., 62
Last, C.G., 60
Learned helplessness, 25
Lehnert, K., 26
Leitenberg, H., 34
Lester, D., 61
Levinson, D., 8, 50, 52, 53, 54, 83
Lewinsohn, P., 73
Lewis, D.O., 9
Lipovsky, J.A., 72
Lockage phenomenon, 38-39, See also
   Intrafamilial homicide
Lockhart, L.L., 18, 88
Lovell, M.L., 78
Lovely, R., 9
Low, H., 7

Luna, A., 5
Lynch, M., 82
Main, M., 28
Maiuro, R.D., 15
Malkin, C.M., 8
Mandatory reporting laws, 65, 66, 70, 78
Mandel, F., 26
Mangold, W.D., 89
March, J.S., 60
Marx, T.J., 3
Mason, R., 12
Matson Evaluation of Social Skills
      (MESSY), 62
Matson, J.L., 62
Mattson, A., 7
Maynard, P.E., 66, 70, 77
McCloskey, L.A., 35, 44
McKnight, C.K., 39
McLeer, S.V., 27
McVicar, D., 82
Media, 84
Mednick, B., 7
Mednick, S.A., 7
Mehregany, D., 30
Meloy, J.R., 15
Methodological issues, 14, 18, 39-40, 51,
      87-89
Miller, T.W., 66
Milner, J.S., 9, 11
Minimal brain dysfunction (MBD), 7, See
      also Biological perspective
Modeling. See Social learning theory
Mohr, J.W., 39
Monahan, J., 16, 82
Moore, J.G., 35, 36
Moos, B.S., 62
Moos, R.H., 62
Moreau, D., 73
Moser, J., 25
Mufson, L., 73
Multidimensional Anxiety Scale for
      Children (MASC), 60
Murdoch, D., 14
Myers, S.A., 15, 20
Nader, K., 40
Neglect, 19, 22, See also Family violence
Neighbors, B., 82
Nelles, W.B., 59

Nesbit, W.C., 46, 49, 84
Neubauer, P.B., 30
Newberger, E.H., 3,4
New York State Child Abuse and
      Maltreatment Register
Nielson, J., 6
Nightingale, N.N., 22
Nonviolence contract, 77-78
Norwood, W.D., 89
O'Leary, K.D., 33, 34, 35, 36, 37, 38, 40,
      45, 47, 48, 58
O'Leary-Porter Scale, 58
Ollendick, T.H., 60
Olson, D.H., 63
Olweus, D., 7
O'Neal, E., 27
Osuna, E., 5, 13
Overholser, J., 26
Owen, D., 7
Paget, K.D., 60, 64
Parental alcohol abuse, 13, 35
Parental conflict, 1-2, 9, 11
Parental personality factors and psychiatric
      disorder, 14-16, 43
Parental unemployment, 11
Parent-child attachment, 28-30, 48
Parker, J.D., 60
Pathological bereavement, 41, 73
Patterson, G.R., 30
Pearson, J., 66
Pediatric social illness, 3, See also family
      violence
Peer relations, 28-30, 31, 62
Pelcovitz, D., 16, 27
Peled, E., 74
Pepping, M., 30
Perrin, S., 60
Peterson, D.R., 59
Petretic-Jackson, P., 28
Pfeffer, C.R., 31
Physical injury, 20-21
Pihl, R.O., 14
Pillemer, K., 41, 42, 43
Pogger, D., 57
Porter, B., 37, 45, 58
Post, S., 39
Post-traumatic stress disorder, 26-27, 40, 72
      See also Internalizing problems

Poznanski, E., 61
Preston, G., 47
Prevention, 51, 82-85
Problem-solving, 11, 74, 79-80, 83
Problem-Solving Communication Training, 79-80
Projective testing, 27, 88
Protective factors, 29, 31 See also Resilience
Psychological abuse. See Psychological maltreatment
Psychological maltreatment
  definition of, 2, 19, 46
  effects of, 12, 48-49, 89
  etiology, 47-48
  parental rejection, 48
  perpetrated by siblings, 31
  prevalence, 47-48
Psychosis, 15, 20
Pugliesi, K.L., 11
Pynoos, R.S., 40
Quay, H.C., 59
Radbill, S.X., 4, 66
Raine, A., 6, 7
Ralph, D., 27
Ray, J.S., 24, 25
RCMAS. See Revised Children's Manifest Anxiety Scale
Reich, W., 59
Reichert, E., 51, 53
Reid, J.C., 10, 31, 48, 61, 71
Renck, M.A., 30
Resilience, 81-82
Reunification, 78
Revised Children's Manifest Anxiety Scale (RCMAS), 60, 64
Revised Fear Survey Schedule for Children (FSSC-R), 60
Reynolds, C.R., 60, 64
Richey, C.A., 78
Richman, N., 31
Richmond, B.O., 60
Robertson, K.R., 9
Robin, A.L., 79
Robinson, C.A., 11
Rodgers, A., 61
Rogers, D.L., 9
Rogosch, 82
Rose, R.M., 7

Rosenbaum, A., 33, 34, 35, 36, 37, 40
Rosenberg, T.K., 10, 61, 71, 81
Ross, D., 14
Ross, M.A., 74
Roter, D., 62
Running away behavior, 37
Rush, A.J., 38
Russell, C.S., 63
Ryan, M.A., 65, 86
Rynerson, B.C., 9
Sack, W.H., 12
Safety skills/issues, 58, 70-71, 74, 75
Salem, P., 66
Salzinger, S., 26, 29, 30
Sandgrund, A., 11, 21
Sandler, J., 69
Sattler, J.M., 61
Saunders, D.G., 69
Sayger, T.V., 62
Scale for Suicide Ideation, 61
Scapegoating, 12, 36, 46
Schalling, D., 7
Schedule for Affective Disorders and Schizophrenia for School-Age Children (K-SADS), 59
Schiavi, P.C., 7
Schotte, D.E., 61
Scmitt, B.D., 68, 69
Schultz-Larsen, J., 6
Self-esteem, 25, 41, 75, 82
Self-Esteem Inventory, 25
Seligman, M.E.P., 25
Shaffer, D., 58
Shaken baby syndrome, 20, See also Physical injury
Shamos, S. 81
Shaw, B.F., 38
Shekim, W.O., 18, 19, 24
Shepherd, J.A., 81
Shepherd, P., 33, 34
Sherick, R.B., 25
Sibling rivalry. See Sibling violence
Sibling violence, 30-31, 49, 52, 85
Silver, H.K., 4
Silver, J.M., 6
Silverman, F.N., 4
Silverman, W.K., 59, 60
Single parenthood, 12, 13

Social development, 28-30, 39
Social exchange theory, 43
Social interactional model, 11, *See also*
    Family systems approaches
Social learning theory, 8, 17, 28, 35, 38, 43
Social support
    as moderating factor, 19
    as protective factor, 54, 81-82
    as risk factor, 24
    increasing, 71-72, 75, 78-79
Sociobiological theory, 7-8
Socioeconomic status (SES), 18, 22, 81, 89
Sonnenberg, S.M., 72
Spanking. *See* Corporal punishment
Spielberger, C.D., 60
Spivak, G., 67
Spousal violence
    cross-culturally, 52
    etiology of, 34-35
    homicide, 35, 40-41
    impact on children, 35-39
    nature of, 33-34
    prevalence of, 34
Spouse abuse. *See* Spousal violence
Sprenkle, D.H., 63
Sroufe, L.A., 68
Stagg, V., 37, 38
Stalking behavior, 15
Stallings, P., 60
Stanford-Binet Intelligence Scale, 61
Starr, R.H., 83
Starzomski, A., 35
State-Trait Anxiety Inventory for Children
    (STAIC), 60
Steele, B.F., 4
Steer, R.A., 61
Steinmetz, S., 18
Stevenson, J., 31
Stith, S.M., 14
Stone, L.A., 28
Straus, M.A., 3, 18, 62, 79
Suh, E.K., 35
Suicidal behaviors and ideation, 26, 38
Sullivan, K., 60
Sulzberger, L.A., 10
Svensson, J., 7
Syers, M., 66

Systemic belief approach, 11, *See also*
    Family systems approaches
Taghizadeh, P., 61
Tarnowski, K.J., 24, 25, 26
Testosterone, 7, *See also* Biological
    perspective
Theilgaard, A., 7
Thoennes, N., 66, 67
Thorndike, R.L., 61
Tilden, V. P., 33, 34, 41, 56
Toedter, L., 28
Treatment. *See* Intervention strategies
Trexler, L., 61
Trichotillomania, 1-2
Turkel, S.B., 86
Turner, T., 34
Twentyman, C.T., 15, 21, 23
Unis, A.S., 25
Valentine, L., 81
van Dalen, A., 70
van Ginkel, C., 35
Veltkamp, L.J., 66
Venables, P.H., 7
Violent female offenders, 89
Violent male offenders, 6-7
Vitalianio, P.P., 15
Vogel, D., 37
Wagner, B.C., 15
Walker, E.F., 22
Walker, L.E., 33, 34
Watson, W.L., 11
Watt, N.F., 81
Wechsler, D., 61
Wechsler Intelligence Scale for Children
    (WISC-III), 61
Wechsler Preschool and Primary Scale of
    Intelligence (WPPSI), 61
Weghorst, S.J., 13
Weiner, M., 26
Weissman, M.M., 61, 73
Wetzel, L., 74
White, D., 7
White, K.M., 3
Widom, C.S., 8, 9-10
Willbach, D., 10, 11, 77, 78,
Williams, M., 7
Williams, O.J., 9, 43
Wills, G.D., 37

Wilson, M.E.H., 62
Wilson, M.I., 13
Wilson, S.K., 22, 37, 38, 39, 58, 74, 76
Wissow, L.S., 62
Wolfe, D.A., 17, 19, 22, 28, 36, 37, 38, 39,
    40, 58, 60, 62, 69, 73, 74, 77, 86
Womens shelters, 5, 36, 37-38, 39-40, 44,
    66
Wright, L.M., 11
Wright, S.A., 48
Yanushefski, A.M., 28

Yates, A., 46
Yde, H., 6
Yeager, C., 9
Yegidis, B.L., 5, 8, 13, 16, 18, 68, 70, 73,
    77, 79
Yo-yo children, 36
Yudofsky, S.C., 6, 69, 70
Yule, W., 72
Zak, L., 22, 37, 38, 39
Zegree, J.B., 15
Zigler, E., 10

ABOUT THE AUTHORS

Javad H. Kashani (M.D.) is Chief, Division of Psychiatry in the Department of Psychiatry and Neurology at the University of Missouri—Columbia. He is also Professor of Psychiatry, Psychology, and Pediatrics as well as Director of Children and Adolescent Services at Mid-Missouri Mental Health Center. His research interests are in the area of child internalizing disorders and family violence, and have resulted in the publication of more than 100 scientific articles. His clinical studies in the last two decades merited him the most prestigious award in child psychiatry in North America—the Blanche F. Ittleson Award (1989).

Wesley D. Allan (M.A., University of Nevada at Las Vegas) is completing his Ph.D. in child clinical psychology at the University of Missouri—Columbia. His major research interests are child internalizing disorders and family violence, and he helped develop the School Anxiety Project, a research and treatment clinic for children with school anxiety, at the University of Missouri—Columbia. He is coauthor of numerous journal articles on child anxiety and depression as well as family abuse among juveniles who commit homicide.